SHE WAS ALWAYS THERE

Also by Signe Eklund Schaefer

I Give You My Word:
Women's Letters as Life support, 1973–1987

Why on Earth?
Biography and the Practice of Human Becoming

More Lifeways:
Finding Support and Inspiration in Family Life
Coeditor with Patti Smith

Ariadne's Awakening:
Taking up the Threads of Consciousness
Coauthor with Margli Matthews and Betty Staley

She Was Always There

Sophia as a Story for Our Time

Signe Eklund Schaefer

SteinerBooks | 2023

SteinerBooks
An imprint of Anthropsophic Press, Inc.
834 Main Street, PO Box 358
Spencertown, New York 12165
www.steinerbooks.org

Design: William Jens Jensen

Library of Congress Control Number: 2023934740

ISBN: 978-1-62148-331-1

Printed in the United States of America

Contents

for

Cyris and Talei

&

Noah and Lela

You give me hope for what will come

This is to be a collection without order, taken from many papers, which I have copied here, hoping afterwards to rearrange them according to the subjects of which they treat; and I believe that I shall have to repeat the same thing several times; for which, O reader, blame me not, because the subjects of the world are many, and memory alone cannot retain them.

Leonardo da Vinci

Another world is not only possible, she is on her way. On a quiet day, I can hear her breathing.

Arundhati Roy

Preface

Not long ago, I saw a documentary on the life of Leonard Cohen that focused on the writing of his much-loved song "Hallelujah." In a moment of reflection, he said, "You look around and you see a world that cannot be made sense of. You either raise your fist or you say Hallelujah." When I heard that, I flashed on my efforts with this book, and I realized that, in the roundabout way of inner intention, my aim was to say Hallelujah (*an expression of rejoicing*) to Sophia.

I have struggled with not wanting to write, as I once knew how to do, a treatise on Sophia, a logical description of how she has been seen throughout the ages, or a case for her importance now. I did not want to write "about" her, but to somehow invite her onto the page. And also, to invite readers to bring their own wonderings into their reading.

It is my experience that Sophia calls me, ever and again, to meet her newly, and not only through my memories or my research and study—not to simply settle into what I think I already know. We meet this dilemma, of course, in all our relationships. How do we allow life and newness into our perceptions of those we know well? This is the work of enkindling interest and staying alive to the people, the ideas, and even the spiritual beings who are part of our biography, our ongoing story. My effort in speaking of Sophia has been to allow, at least occasionally, my words to hover at the edge of language and consciousness, to make space for her presence in our considerations. The word *diffuse* was used by one kind reader, which I understand, although I have not necessarily made things more precise. I have not been looking for fixed answers but for a living dialogue with mystery.

Each of the three chapters speaks in a somewhat different voice. As I was writing, I tended to think of them as: 1) my story, 2) her story, and 3) our story. Of course, they inevitably interweave. In many ways this is an idiosyncratic book; it comes out of questions I have lived with for many decades. The basic themes could have gone in many different directions. And I hope this will still happen, within readers and in conversations with others.

I am very aware of the many social, scientific, literary, and mythic depths that are not addressed here. I can imagine readers saying, "How could you have left out...?" It has been hard for me not to lament the missing subject areas and the parts of Sophia's story that I have indeed left out of this small book. There is a bibliography at the end listing wonderful sources for further study. I have intended my words as an offering toward each reader's own ongoing questions into these times we live in.

Rudolf Steiner's Anthroposophy has been central in my journey toward understanding myself and the world. He also referred to his work as spiritual science, and it is an exploration into the far reaches of the wisdom of the world. This is Sophia's realm, and I want my words to celebrate her presence and our searching. I close these introductory words with a thought from Steiner:

> ...we must not see spiritual science as something to which we devote a few passing thoughts. In fact, it is one of the most necessary prerequisites for the recovery of our public life. As a pragmatist, I know what people will say—that they have jobs; they have to work; and they don't have enough time to devote to something as complex as spiritual science. On the other hand, no matter how busy we are today, we cannot avoid noticing that we are treading on a slippery slope. Does what we are busy doing simply help lead the way into chaos? Don't we really need to devote every hour we can spare to radical prospects for recovery?

Signe Eklund Schaefer
Great Barrington, Massachusetts
January 2023

It's Time

The cabin floor swept
the windows washed
She smiles
seeing these worthy tasks
to delay the real step
She is a whisper in my heart
un-worded still
while I stay cautious
worrying about fixing too soon
though an echo laughs
hardly too soon
rather a lifetime of listening
watching her weave
everywhere
She knows I honor her
even in my silence
but lately I hear moaning
something labors to be born

Chapter 1
Musings on Sophia

We must carefully distinguish between object and name. We must not allow ourselves to be deceived into thinking that by giving a certain name to a being we have at the same time experienced and felt this being in the right way.

—RUDOLF STEINER

This is a book devoted to Sophia. Readers have a right to ask: Who, or perhaps what, is she? It is the difficulty of answering that question that has kept me from writing for many years, except in momentary musings that might catch a brief glimpse of her presence. Any concise answer about her feels inadequate. She is a great wisdom being who embraces human becoming in all its striving and suffering. She is known as a divine feminine reality from before the division into feminine and masculine. She is an archetypal maternal being bearing all that was, and is, and will be. And now she seems to be approaching our ongoing human story in new ways, calling us to a new step in our awakening consciousness.

It is difficult to talk about spiritual being(s) in our materialistic age. To some it can seem odd, or quaint, or even deluded. And yet, naming the reality around us matters; it is part of our human legacy. In everyday life, we ask quite naturally: What flower is that? What is the name of that river we floated down years ago? What is your baby's name? We are not satisfied to remain with just *flower, river, baby*—much less to refer simply to a generic *thing*.

For as long as I can remember, I have had a feeling for—I would even say I have *known*—intangible sources of inspiration, comfort, and challenge. I know I am not alone with this experience. Raised outside of any religious tradition, I had no names for these realities, though I never doubted them. One I called "the Lady." I do not remember when this started, but since I was young "she" was there, a knocking presence in my heart, an invisible part of my consciousness, wordlessly offering encouragement and support.

When I was twenty and in my last year of college, I heard about the Austrian scientist and spiritual teacher Rudolf Steiner and the work he called *Anthroposophia*, or in English, Anthroposophy. Something resounded deep within me. Later, as I began to read his descriptions of different spiritual beings, I remember thinking, "Oh, so this is what that is called." I began to feel the possibility of discovering names for some of my inner experiences.

It did not take long for me to see how my deepening study of Anthroposophy aligned with my growing interest in the women's movement—this was in the late 1960s and early '70s. In particular, I found myself drawn to a divine feminine presence that both people interested in Steiner and women researching early matriarchal influences would sometimes refer to as Sophia. I learned through exploring different mythologies that this great wisdom being had borne many other names throughout the ages—The Great Mother, Isis, Tiamet, Gaia, Mary, Kuan Yin, Aditi, Ala, Skywoman, to mention only a few.

Names can clothe realities and give them strength, but they can also become binding. Identification can bring attention and understanding, but we can also fall asleep into what someone is called and forget that there is a living being who bears that name. We can rest too easily in fixed images. The wonderful thing about the word *being*—as in spiritual being or human being—is that it is not only a noun, the name of a particular entity, but it is also a verb, suggesting ongoing becoming.

When I think of spiritual beings, I remember a sentence by Rudolf Steiner in which he states, "Everyone resembles the god he (she/they) understands."[1] When people try to understand an invisible reality for which they have a living feeling, it is perhaps inevitable that what lives in their imaginations from the sense world will be brought to bear on their portrayals of divine beings. The resemblance goes both ways. Part of the dilemma of our materialistic times is that, when we have no understanding of a world beyond what can be measured, weighed and calculated, we are left with little to resemble that offers inspiration beyond what we already know about our sense-based selves.

I am aware that some readers will enter easily into a discussion of spiritual beings, while others may balk at this invitation. I can understand a resistance to the use of names that carry the weight of religious tradition that has become clouded through the centuries. And yet, these traditions, like the ancient myths before them, each speak a certain truth—however limited or one-sided—about how people at different times and in different parts of the world understood themselves and their relationship to what they perceived as a divine world.

Putting aside for a moment the question of names, it is always possible—and, I would say, also necessary—to ask into one's own experiences in life. Have there been times when you felt a presence, a sense of movement or activity that could not be explained by logic or common sense or physical calculation? Perhaps this appeared as an intuition, a kind of sounding to which you listened and knew that it came in some way from beyond your normal intellectual grasp. Perhaps it resounded as an inner voice, or in a dream or waking thought, or as an intrusion into the otherwise busyness of your mind, and you knew that you were experiencing something true. You trusted your knowing in that moment. This may also have been accompanied by a feeling that what was happening did not belong to just you and was not only your own creation.

We may gratefully receive such an experience, or we might try to dismiss it as fantasy. We may feel confused at how to articulate, even just to ourselves, what happened. Was it real? What actually occurred? How do we conceptualize such phenomena? In a moment like this we can feel the inadequacy of our language to describe an experience that is somehow beyond matter.

I have come to see such moments as experiences at the threshold between the everyday world of the senses and the invisible—but always there—reality of the spirit. For a moment, the veil between these worlds thins, and we are offered something from across the threshold. We may choose to connect our perception to what we might call angels or other helpful divine beings. More problematically, we might experience powerful and frightening adversarial beings. Perhaps we sense the presence of loved ones who have died. I find myself interested in the variety of ways that what I perceive as spirit can present itself, and I find it helpful to consider that different spiritual beings are infusing my life with meaning, challenge, and support. Even as I feel the unity of the divine world, I find it necessary to be open to various distinct expressions of spiritual activity.

What is present in these pages has been living in me for many years. Each time I would consider actually formulating my questions and ideas in writing, I would find myself challenged by the impossibility of expressing, in a way that felt true to me, what I have come to recognize with the name Sophia. As the wisdom of the world, she is all-comprehensive. To give one characterization is to leave out its opposite, which also belongs to the totality of her being. Considering her can land us in the realm of paradox, asking us to take an ever-wider view. In recent years there have been many fine books written about Sophia. I knew I did not want to present one more case for her—an intellectual explication to prove her existence. But how to express this being who is so much more than a "subject" of inquiry?

Finally, I decided that I would forego the idea of a straightforward narrative and instead interweave musings, poems, saved quotations, and other assorted notes from my many years of living with questions about and to her. She shows up everywhere in my sporadic journals—sometimes directly, sometimes in a margin as a question (*Is she illusive? Or am I asleep? Is it more about lifting the veil—or about knowing her? Is there a difference?*). Some of my journal entries have dates, other writings are on scraps of paper whose context at the time I no doubt thought I would remember, but no longer do. So, I am letting different musings find their own progression, sharing dates where I can but knowing that there is a timelessness to my long, and still ongoing, search.

~

JOURNAL—UNDATED

The more we try to talk of her—define her, name her—the more evasive she becomes... we can characterize, we can innumerate qualities (wisdom, compassion, truth, service, love...) but we cannot catch her. Luckily, she is not to be captured, but to be allowed, participated with, invited, appreciated.... She will not be turned into a thing. (Things are products of our patriarchal distinctions once we fell away from original participation.) Now, as individuals recognize others and new possibilities of community, we come again toward her mystery.

~

JOURNAL—UNDATED

I have friends who are deeply into the mythology of Sophia and the multicultural stories of this divine feminine presence. I have other friends who have no idea what I am talking about if I refer to her. Some love the intellectual mystery of trying to place her in a cosmological pantheon, while others hope to commune with her on a moonlit night. Still others, on the grounds of their very respectable secular humanism reject the very idea of any non-physical beings, or they seek explanations for confusing experiences in the latest brain research.

And I? It's difficult for me to articulate what I feel, what I know without adequate words. I can enter conversations about her stories, which I have explored for decades. But that is not where I seek her now. The wonderful myths are background, perhaps I could also say foundational, but the being I would speak of now exists in a contemporary reality. She is of the present, not the past. Is it our—my—inadequate vision, or imagination, that cannot perceive her current formless form, or find the words to clothe her presence or her mission?

Of course, I know that no words can capture divine beings. The very wish of "capture" points out the flaw in such a search. Instead, we characterize around and around—hopefully, controlling our self-importance and pretension. I feel my own inadequacy at cross purposes with my long-devoted search and with my wish to open up the questions that might let her live within us, that might help us recognize and dare to name her evolving truth.

~

WORDS ON WAKING—UNDATED

"Why is She? How is She? Not—What is She?"

Is this to get away from the idea of her as a "thing," even a noun? Is she a verb?

~

Often my words to or from Sophia have come as a poem. I did not consider myself a poet, but for decades words have arrived this way, more easily than in definitive statements. The language of poetry allows flexibility and invites associations. It reaches over boundaries of grammar and logic. I share some of these poems offered to her illusive being not for their literary merit, but because they helped me take hold of a moment's experience.

~

JOURNAL—6/11/86

In doing spiritual research, what does it mean that the object/idea of interest commands the method of investigation—i.e., it has its own right way, which we have to discover?

~

For Sophia

"Knowing you are there"

The line comes with waking
as a title to nothing I intended to
write
yet here I am and writing.

I feel you in the wings
of my inconstant consciousness.
It seems presumptuous
to think you wait for me,
rather I sense

I am waiting for myself
for the moment
when I gather
all I hold of you
and lift the veil
your breath blows clearly through.

10/27/2018

~

I struggle with the question of why one person's musings and meanderings should matter to anyone else. And yet I know that I longed for some of the Sophia scholars, whose work I deeply appreciated, to step away from their authoritative voices and tell me why they cared so much about this subject. I wanted to know how Sophia entered their journeys of intellectual inquiry, how she lived in them. When authors did reveal small pieces of themselves, I was so grateful. My wish in sharing my own evolving process is to encourage readers to take your own ponderings seriously and to trust your questions and recognitions.

My conscious searching for Sophia began when I became a mother in my early twenties. Accompanying my love for my baby was a longing to know more about what it meant to be a mother. Up until then I had known myself as a daughter, a student, a friend, a wife...but now a whole new dimension of reality opened up for me, and it was filled with a deep sense of responsibility. By twenty-five I had a second child, and a new question had become clear: "Why is my 'I' a woman now?" I asked this from my feeling for the truth of reincarnation, and in the knowledge that in some way an eternal part of myself, existing beyond any division into female/male, had intended a mighty learning for this lifetime—as a woman, as a mother—and especially so in a time when questions about women's liberation were active in the world and within me.

I felt the importance of the developing women's movement, but my particular questions went beyond the need for greater rights and better career opportunities. I wanted to know what was happening at a deeper level of human development: what feminine qualities were calling out to be given more space, more value?—in women certainly, but not only. I felt there was a critical need for a new balancing between masculine and feminine qualities as they were playing out in society and in each individual soul. I did not see this as only about readjusting the roles of men and women, but of awakening with conscious responsibility to long suppressed desires and possibilities that could contribute in quite new ways toward a much-needed balancing in the social order, in family lives and in the maturing of individuals of any gender.

~

JOURNAL—10/3/2003

To Know—to enter, to understand. All my life I've wanted to know—more than the obvious, the why of things, background, reason, the who of another. Knowing isn't essentially about information for me, though information may be needed. It goes deeper, broader than that—it's not the facts, but the act of connection—to what's true, what's real, what matters. It follows wondering—it needs wandering. It has moments of aha! but it never feels finished.

~

Why be a Woman?

Eva–woman took the apple
and we came down.
Now ages past we will again ascend,
reaching for the source, with ego force
that gift of sacrifice—
becoming each one's own in long lives'
struggling.
And for this task we are as women now
needing bodies softer,
open, chalice-like,
that we may know, and bear, and love
this upward working.

February 1980

~

For several years this effort to understand feminine and masculine became a central focus of my personal development, my study, and my emerging work. Conversations with women friends led to forming women's groups, naming our work Ariadne after the maiden in Greek mythology, offering public workshops and conferences, publishing an international newsletter, and eventually writing a book.[2] We looked into our own life experiences, read widely in feminist literature, and studied myths from around the world. So many myths began with creative goddess figures who eventually yielded to or were replaced by male heroes in what was often referred to as the Patriarchal Revolution. We felt strongly that our current times were asking for new attention to whatever the feminine side of our human nature might bring as a balancing force to the masculine one-sidedness we experienced in the culture at large, in working life, in relationships, and also within ourselves.

~

JOURNAL—2/22/94

Sophia cannot be coming only that women should experience her—though we must. The need is beyond gender differences, even as gender consciousness helps us to recognize the need.

~

From a letter to a friend—8/30/1987

Next weekend is a meeting of people who want to develop the questions raised by Ariadne. We should be a group of about 8 or 10 and we will focus on the Isis/Maria/Sophia being as a background to any work on a renewal of the feminine. It's always such a challenge to balance the deepest, most esoteric questions with the real practical societal needs. But this is a group of women who see this theme as a central part of our work (whatever that may be—teacher of adults, or little kids, curative work, parent work, etc.).

~

Since the 1970s, I had been reading creation stories and myths from different parts of the world. Although there were almost always great mother figures present from the beginnings of time, I initially found very few references to the name Sophia, except as Wisdom in ancient Greece, with the development of philosophy (Philo-Sophia—love of Wisdom), and then in the Wisdom literature of the Bible where she is referred to as a partner to the Father God, before creation. I was looking for her, but when I would check the index in many of the books that began to be published about the divine feminine, I did not find much. She was referred to by the Gnostics, and later by Alchemists, but even within the feminist scholarship of that time, she was rarely addressed. Then in 1991 two very fine books were published: *The Myth of the Goddess: Evolution of an Image*, by Anne

Baring and Jules Cashford, and *Sophia: Goddess of Wisdom*, by Caitlin Matthews.

~

FROM *SOPHIA: GODDESS OF WISDOM*
BY CAITLIN MATTHEWS

Sophia is a guerilla combat Goddess, attired in camouflage veils so complete that many orthodox spiritualities never realized that the Goddess was still accompanying them.

~

Sometime in the late 1970s, I read a book by F. W. Zeylmans van Emmichoven on Rudolf Steiner's "Foundation Stone,"[3] the meditation that Steiner spoke at the founding of the Anthroposophical Society in 1923. In the final chapters of this book, the author referred to a new myth that Steiner had told in 1918, in a series of lectures later published as *Ancient Myths*.[4] I was struck by what I read and went in search of this new myth.

Referred to as the *New Isis Myth*, it is a strange story. It is not about the ancient Egyptian Isis, but rather is a story of and for our times, about her new state as a contemporary goddess figure who is closely connected with the human being. In my first readings I found the images mysterious and provocative. I could not quite understand what the story was "about," but even so, I knew I had found something vitally important for my life.

I soon came to understand that Steiner connected the Goddess Isis of ancient Egypt with the being of Sophia, and that he had spoken in a variety of settings about the importance for contemporary humanity to come to know this being in her present form. He spoke of this with some urgency in a series of lectures given in 1920, when he stated directly that we need to fulfill a new Isis/Sophia myth for our times.[5]

Over the many decades since first discovering this myth, I have told it in many diverse settings, and I have come to see how it truly is a story for today. There are images of being asleep, of misplaced love, of questionable paternity, and the lack of understanding the true nature of an offspring. There is the power of technology, cloned beings with the appearance of life, but obeying only mechanical laws, and there is an uneasy relationship between ancient mystery wisdom and modern science. There is much else as well, and most central is the gradual awakening to a new capacity of living spiritual perception. This is a story of a divine being who identifies with the human being and who issues a call to all of us to lift her veil.

Here is a telling of Rudolf Steiner's *New Isis/Sophia Myth*, in my own words, but very close to his original.

—

The New Isis/Sophia Myth

The story takes place in the land of the Philistines, in the age of scientific profundity. On a secluded hill, there was a remarkable building that was open to visitors at convenient times, even though few people noticed it at all. In a central place in the building was a large statue of the Representative of Humanity surrounded by adversarial beings, one type who would lift us away from our earthly responsibilities and another who would grind us ever more tightly into matter. (In the story they are specifically named Lucifer and Ahriman.) This statue, however, was actually a veil for another, invisible statue—behind the visible statue was a statue of the New Isis, the Isis of a new age.

Some people in this age of abstract and symbolical thinking determined that the visible statue represented or signified the New Isis, but this only showed their complete lack of real understanding. The figures in the visible statue were artistic renderings of their own true realities—they were what they appeared to be—and behind them was the real, although invisible, New Isis.

In special circumstances a few visitors had experienced the New Isis behind the visible statue and had seen that she was asleep. At special moments some were able to read the inscription that stood clearly there: "I am the Human Being, I am the Past, the Present, and the Future. Every mortal should lift my veil." This was a significant change from an inscription that once accompanied a veiled statue of Isis in ancient Egypt. The earlier inscription had read: "I am the All. I am the Past, the Present, and the Future; no mortal has yet lifted my veil." The New Isis, identifying as she now does with all humanity, calls clearly for every mortal to lift her veil.

One day, and then again and again, another figure approached the sleeping New Isis, somewhat like a visitor. And she considered this visitor to be her benefactor, and she loved him. One day both the New Isis and her visitor believed in a particular illusion: she had an offspring and she considered her visitor to be the father. He also thought he was the father, although he was not. This visiting spirit was, in fact, the New Typhon. The old Typhon, a force of darkness in ancient Egypt, had also been known then as Seth. This New Typhon believed that if he took possession of the New Isis, he would secure a special increase in his worldly power.

The New Isis had an offspring, but she understood nothing of its nature. She moved it around, dragged it into far off lands because she thought that this was what she must do. She trailed her offspring through different regions of the world until it fell into fourteen pieces, through the very power of the world.

When the New Typhon became aware of how the New Isis had dragged her offspring about until the world had broken it into fourteen pieces, he gathered the pieces together into a single whole. With his vast scientific knowledge and technological skills, he made a single being again out of the fourteen pieces, but this being obeyed only the laws of the machine. It appeared to have life but it obeyed only mechanical laws, and because it had arisen out of fourteen pieces, it could reproduce itself fourteen-fold. And the New Typhon could give an image of his own countenance to each one. Now each of the fourteen apparent offspring of the New Isis resembled the being of the New Typhon.

And the New Isis had to watch all these strange events, half-divining the miraculous changes that had occurred, aware that she had dragged her offspring about and that she had somehow brought all this to pass. Then one day she was able to receive her offspring once again in its true form. She received it back in its genuine form from a group of nature spirits, from nature elementals. Her offspring had been stamped into the offspring of the New Typhon only through an illusion, and now as she received it back in its true form, a tremendous, clairvoyant vision dawned upon her: she realized that although she had become a New Isis, she was still wearing the cow horns of ancient Egypt.

The power of her clairvoyance now summoned perhaps the New Typhon himself, although some say Mercury, and through the strength of her clairvoyance he was obliged to place a crown on her head, to set it where the old crown that Horus had seized from her so long ago had been, in fact on the spot where the cow horns now stood. But this new crown was only of paper, covered with all sorts of scientific information, and yet it was of paper. So now the New Isis had two crowns on her head, the cow horns and the paper crown adorned with all the knowledge and data of the age.

One day, through the strength of her clairvoyance, there arose within her the deep meaning, "as far as the age could reach," of what is described as the Logos in the Gospel of St. John. The deep meaning of the Mystery of Golgotha arose within her. Through the strength of this mystery, the power of the cow horns took hold of the paper crown and transformed them both into a golden crown of genuine wisdom.

~

Can we recognize our times, and perhaps even ourselves, in the provocative images of this story? Does the call to lift the veil resonate within us? How do we awaken within the many challenges we face—as individuals and as members of the society in which we live, and even beyond that, as participants in the future becoming of the earth? After telling the myth, Rudolf Steiner spoke these words: *Even though the power of action that is bound up with the new Isis statue is at first weak, exploring, and tentative, it is to be the starting point of something that is deeply justified in the impulses of the modern age, deeply justified in what this age is meant to become and must become.*[6]

I will return to further considerations of the New Isis/Sophia myth in chapter 3.

~

She Who Is There and Everywhere

Invisible being I know your
knocking
strong beating from within my heart
I am too eager to open the door
it jams and the key forgotten.

I wander like you, searching
grieving for a better world
not knowing where I go
and fearing to lose the ones I love.

Still
you drop a precious pearl
as gift to my pondering heart
a sudden knowing:
why drag so much around?
So many pieces fill my busy heart
too full to hear
your ever-present call
behind the familiar veil.
Lady Wisdom
your knocking wakes
and makes me
if I will.

TORONTO, 2000

~

Many years ago, I visited Chartres Cathedral in France. I knew this to be a special place, built on the site of an ancient mystery center and never quite adhering to traditional Catholic doctrine. Wherever you look, in the statuary and in the magnificent stained-glass windows, there are stories being told. These vibrant and detailed imaginations show tales from the Bible for the illiterate worshippers of the Middle Ages. There are female images everywhere; indeed, the cathedral is filled with representations of the Virgin Mary, of course, but I would also say Sophia, with the Christ Child enthroned on her lap. The architecture and imagery, the geometry, the forms and colors seemed to me an embodiment in the 12th and 13th centuries of the wisdom of the world, as perceived by the many artisans and craftspeople who worked at constructing the cathedral.

One sculpture, in a pointed niche high up above the doors on the right side of the South Portal, facing the town, has stayed with me throughout the years. Perhaps it has been deemed too insignificant to appear in books about Chartres, but I stood amazed when I saw it. The image belongs to the reason I am writing this book. There is a seated female figure, and she is holding an open book. What struck me so forcefully was that she is not reading the book. Rather she holds it open, facing it outward toward the people far below. The book of wisdom is open, waiting to be read by us.

~

Chartres—July 6, 2000

1.
Lady of my heart
I see you here in stone
stone intoning
the rhythms of your being.
How many bodies have you worn?
The old stories offered abode
and told of you
as water, night,
or a mighty tree.
As goddess we have known you
and shown you
throne crowned
or carrying the sprouted corn
your book ever opening
though our eyes became veiled.
Now here this majesty of stone
and glass
of movement and light
within the darkness:
it all embodies you.
And your image is everywhere
birthing the child
the throned child

who is to rule us all:
"I am" within
I am within you now
within your eternal embrace.
2.
And still
my search goes on.
This beautiful body
this cathedral gown
you can at will
still wear
seems not your present size.
Where are you now?
I hear you call in words
that found my heart anew.
The veil shifts
I glean I am
forming from within
while without
your green still greens
and your miracle blue
embraces everything.
Your red is communion
the outpouring and inbreathing
of hearts.

3.
Lady, today I name you Love.

~

In the next chapter we will follow some of the pathways this mighty wisdom being has wandered through the ages, her story interweaving in myriad ways with our own evolving human becoming.

There is in all visible things an invisible fecundity,
a dimmed light, a meek namelessness,
a hidden wholeness.
This mysterious Unity and Integrity is Wisdom,
the Mother of all, Natura naturans.
There is in all things an inexhaustible
sweetness and purity,
a silence that is a fount of action and joy.
It rises up in wordless gentleness
and flows out to me
from the unseen roots of all created being,
welcoming me tenderly,
saluting me with indescribable humility.
This is at once my own being, my own nature,
and the Gift of my Creator's Thought and Art
within me, speaking as Hagia Sophia,
speaking as my sister,
Wisdom . . .

THOMAS MERTON
from *Hagia Sophia*
(1. Dawn. The Hour of Lauds)

Chapter 2
Divine Wisdom and Her Travails

A short telling of a very long story
that could have taken many different turnings.

—

When did it happen? Where did it happen?
When and where did it not happen?

Once upon a time, before time as we know it, there appeared a mighty Egg, a Cow, the Waters, or the Night, perhaps a World Womb, a Great Round, or the Great Mother of All. She was there as feminine being before division, experienced everywhere, divine and whole, and birthing the world into existence.

For unknown ages she brooded a future human race. Gradually men and women came into being and the earth took on its evolving form. There were mountains and rivers, forests and plains. In time people walked the earth, and they carved intricate figurines in stone and bone and ivory. Round honoring of her, full-bellied and ready to give birth. The people left these offerings in caves, deep within Her earth womb, to rest for 15,000 or 35,000 years and more, to wait for eyes that might see her in a new light. And the walls of some caves were adorned with animals who were also part of her. Everything was in relationship, belonging to a grand encompassing unity. She had no known male partners.

Many thousands of years would go by before her story would be told in ways that became remembered, before she would arise in myths around the world, speaking of origins and also showing the people the mysteries of agriculture and the domestication of animals, the arts of spinning and weaving, and the forming of pots from clay. There were remnants of her civilizing influence, more than 10,000 years old, throughout Old Europe, as well as at Çatal Höyük in southern Anatolia, Turkey. She was the Great Mother of birth and death and regeneration, bestowing a gradual recognition and celebration of rhythm and order in the people's experience of the cycle of the seasons and of human life itself.

She prevailed as a Great Mother for long ages, but in the times when her stories began to be remembered, there came a shadow on her bearing. Gradually a son or a brother appeared, and sometimes she would take one as consort. Eventually he would want to exert his might, to dim her light, and to limit her power.

More than 5,000 years ago, during what some call the Bronze Age, myths and hymns about her were appearing in many parts of the world. The stories began to be written down—hieroglyphs on the walls of temples, markings on delicate papyrus or clay tablets. She was still revered as the Great Goddess, but she began to be differentiated with brothers and sisters, daughters and sons. In many lands, and by many names, the people told of her descent into the darkness of the underworld to seek a loved one who had become separated from her and the world of light.

In Samaria, She was called Inanna, while in Babylonia She was known as Ishtar. Her divine being encompassed heaven and earth. She bore the crescent moon on her head, echoing the connection to the moon and the bull horns of the ancient goddess before her, she who was sky, earth and underworld. Inanna was honored with great reverential titles: Queen of Heaven and Earth, Priestess of Heaven, Light of the World, Morning and Evening Star, First Daughter of the Moon, Loud Thundering Storm, Righteous Judge, Forgiver of Sins, Holy Shepherdess, Hierodule of Heaven, Opener of the Womb, Framer of all Decrees, The Amazement of the Land.[7] Complete in herself, the Virgin Goddess manifested in the fertility and unity of plant, animal, and human life. She was a lunar goddess ordering the rhythmic waxing and waning of the moon, and the cycling of life and death. But as the years went by, the myths begin to shift until the god who was once his mother's son sought to achieve domination as a father god.

Human communal life was also slowly changing. Even as the myths began to tell of a jealous brother or an ambitious son beginning to do battle with the all-powerful Mother, the social order in parts of the known world was transforming. Nomadic warrior tribes with their sky and thunder gods swept in from the North and from the East, destroying the peaceful, goddess-worshipping towns of Old Europe. Rivalries and warfare sprang up in many places, and small peaceful villages transformed into walled cities. Death was experienced less as a rightful part of the cycle of life and increasingly as something to be feared.

As warfare grew throughout the land, She sometimes came to be known as a goddess of war, bringing death and destruction to her own creations within the ordering of society. Her wisdom still shone with a principle of justice, but on earth the power of kings, indeed the very idea of power, was growing.

And so, in Samaria the people heard of her son-lover Dumuzi-Tammuz and his death and resurrection. Half-divine, half-human, he died into the underworld like the vegetation over which he was lord. And Inanna-Ishtar made her mourning descent to resurrect him and bring regeneration to the land. Different places told different details of this tale but always there was ritual sacrifice, lamentation, and seasonal resurrection.

In Egypt, from before 3000 BCE, the goddess was known as Isis, and she was a great civilizing force along with her brother Osiris, who was also her spouse. Together they embodied the gradually evolving conception of life for the Egyptian people of that time. The divine world was being addressed in ever more differentiated ways, and so Isis was in time understood as the goddess of 1,000 names, many holding sacred connections to the animal world. Isis herself was revered for over 3,000 years. She was the Great Goddess of the Universe from whom all were born, and also one of the four children of Nut and Geb, who created the Sky and the Earth. Her stories were many, and the contradictions a modern mind might find confusing were not a problem in those long-ago ages when she ruled. Her stories were so well known by word of mouth that nowhere were they all collected until the second century CE, by the Greek writer Plutarch.

Isis and Osiris embodied the ever-renewing round of life and death in the cycle of the year: she was the earth made fertile by his flooding water as it burst the banks of the mighty Nile each year. Her fields were ready to become pregnant with new life and resurrection. But their jealous brother Seth (known later as Typhon), who was the scorching heat and desert wind, would bring drought and blowing sands in an annual reminder of the struggle between growth and devastation. Jealous Seth was that force of antagonism forever threatening life, goodness, and the unity of creation.

One dark day Osiris was tricked by Seth and encased in a beautifully decorated wooden chest carved perfectly to fit only his divine form. As they heard of this entombing of Osiris into physicality, the Egyptian people felt themselves waking up in their own earthly reality. The sealed casket was tossed into the Nile, and mighty Isis, the soul of the world, began a long search for her lost lord. With her hair cut short, and dressed in mourning clothes, she wandered weeping through the land until at Byblos in Phoenicia she heard of a wondrously fragrant tamarisk tree, which had grown around the chest. Disguised as an old woman she sought out the tree, only to find that it had been cut down and taken to be a central pillar in the nearby palace. She sat by a well where maidens of the queen would come to collect water, and she began to gently braid their hair, surrounding them with her fragrant breath. When they returned to the palace, the queen was astonished by this remarkable perfume, and she sent for the strange, veiled woman and asked that she become a nursemaid to her child.

As evening would arrive, mighty Isis would place the sleeping child into the fire, that he might burn away his earthly self and so become an immortal. She would change herself into a swallow and fly grieving round the mighty pillar that enveloped her beloved lord. But one night the queen entered the room and in great distress pulled her little son from the flames, thus preventing him from becoming divine. Now Isis revealed herself in all her magnificence, and from the tall pillar she removed the casket containing Osiris's body. Taking this chest with her, she sailed away, hovering over Osiris in the form of a kite, her great wings endowing him with a kind of life. And she conceived her hawk-headed son, who would be called Horus.

Once when Isis was away caring for her son, Seth discovered the casket hidden among the reeds of a remote marsh. He grabbed the body of Osiris and tore it into fourteen pieces, which he then scattered throughout the land. So, Isis again began her sorrowful searching, and each time she would find one of the pieces of Osiris's body, she would bury it into the earth with reverent ceremony. With this the people of Egypt understood that Osiris was still with them, now working in the underworld where they would meet him when they died, where he would judge their souls in balance with the feather of truth.

Meanwhile Seth's darkness and devastation fell upon the land, and eventually Horus did battle with his uncle over who should be crowned the new King. As brother to Isis the Great Mother Queen, Seth felt entitled to assume the throne. However, times were changing, and matrilineal inheritance was yielding to the new order of patriarchy. And so, Isis convinced the council of gods that Horus should be the next King, not as her son, but because he was the son of Osiris. In this deed Isis herself evolved from Great Mother Goddess to Good Mother. Horus's regency brought a kind of resurrection to Osiris, and from this time onward, the Pharaohs were no longer known as the sons of Isis, but as the sons of Horus.

Horus captured and imprisoned his uncle Seth, but Isis released him. In her infinite wisdom she knew that even the spirit of limitation had a place within the all. Horus had new power, but less wisdom. In a rage at his mother, he ripped off her throne-like crown, replacing it with cow horns. Could he have dimly known how these cow horns echoed the much earlier manifestation of the goddess?

For over 3,000 thousand years and throughout many lands—even into Greece and reaching through the Roman Empire as far as the Danube and the Rhine, Isis continued to be revered. As late as the second century CE, she appeared in the book *The Golden Ass*, written by the Roman philosopher Apuleius, who was also an initiate of her lingering Mysteries. Through his words she still declared her majesty and the reach of her influence:

> ...I am Nature, the universal Mother, mistress of all the elements, primordial child of time, sovereign of all things spiritual, queen of the dead, queen also of the immortals, the single manifestation of all gods and goddesses that are. My nod governs the shining heights of Heaven, the wholesome sea-breezes, the lamentable silences of the world below. Though I am worshipped in many aspects, known by countless names, and

propitiated with all manner of different rites, yet the whole round earth venerates me ...[8]

There is a paradox in Isis, for she was adored as the Great Mother of Life, Death and Regeneration yet she also suffered trial and loss like human beings, and this may explain her lasting appeal. Of all the Egyptian goddesses, only Isis has an individual character and a personal story. As an identifiable "person," as well as a sister, wife and mother, she brings the image of the universal mother an entirely new dimension. Like Inanna in Mesopotamia, so Isis in Egypt relates humanity to the unknowable face of divinity by becoming personal, we might almost say human. She is the mediator between the two realms, as the Virgin Mary was to be for many people thousands of years later. (Anne Baring and Jules Cashford)[9]

In the Babylonian *Enūma Eliš*, the Mother Goddess was known as Tiamat—She who bore all. But as time passed, she became painted in ever-darker tones, as Chaos, Night, and the Primal Salt Water. She came to be seen as demoniacal, an enveloping, smothering force of darkness. In time her grandson Marduk rose up to cleave her in two and so create Heaven and Earth. Now the Mother Goddess was vanquished, and a god of sun, sky and wind assumed rulership. A new creation myth was to be born.

With the coming of the Iron Age (±1200 BCE), the original androgynous and peaceful nature of the Great Mother had been transformed into Maternal and Paternal power and values. Feminine and masculine qualities were now strongly differentiated: *What was feminine was the dragon-mother, the earth and moon, darkness, chaos, confusion, nature as emptied of spirit; and what was masculine was the sky-father, the heaven and sun, light, order, clarity, spirit as freed from nature.*[10] The balance within the sacred marriage could not endure the rising supremacy of the emerging father god, he who created what he brought into being from outside and on his own, who exerted absolute control over what he so masterfully wrought. Spirit and matter would gradually be experienced as a duality, no longer as living aspects of the divine mother's essential being of bearing and relationship.

In Greece as well, male gods wrestled for greater influence, and the leading spirit of them all was Zeus. On the island of Crete echoes of the Great Mother lived longer than on the mainland, although there, too, was a shifting of the dynamics between the older maternal ways and a growing patriarchal power. Legends told of the birth of Zeus and other Greek gods and goddesses in caves on the island, caves adorned with echoes of the much earlier cave paintings in France and elsewhere. Here within Mother

Earth a new cycle of gods and goddesses came into being.

And yet, on Crete the Great Goddess was still to be found in the vibrant frescos, seals, and sculpture of the Minoan people. Her influence was seen among the many images of her significance: bull horns, lions, flying birds, coiling snakes, buzzing bees, and poppy pods bursting with seeds. Here she lingered as the revered Great Mother of Life. Even during the third and second millennia BCE, there were no warriors, no violence, represented in Minoan art, and still no defensive walls around Cretan towns.

This harmonious life on Crete gradually began to change under the rule of King Minos, son of mighty Zeus, and his wife Queen Pasiphaë, she who was a daughter of the Sun god Helios and who still carried an echo of connection to the Great Goddess. Poseidon, God of the sea, was angry with Minos, and in revenge he plotted a dalliance between Pasiphaë and a great white bull. From this she bore a son, the Minotaur, who had the body of a man but the head of a bull. King Minos could not kill his Queen's offspring because of her lingering goddess connection; but in order to hide him away, he had Daedalus build a mighty labyrinth from which the monster could not escape. One day the young hero Theseus arrived on Crete, as part of a tribute from Athens owed to King Minos—seven youths and seven maidens destined to be led into the labyrinth where they would be devoured by the Minotaur. Ariadne, the daughter of Minos and Pasiphaë, watched Theseus being paraded through Knossos with the other Athenians and determined to save him. From Daedalus she obtained a golden thread that Theseus could tie to the entrance of the labyrinth and so go in, slay the monster and rewind the thread to find his way back out. In gratitude he took Ariadne with him as he sailed back to Athens. But soon he left her asleep on the isle of Naxos as he sailed off to new heroic adventures. Though bereft by this betrayal, Ariadne was soon comforted by the god Dionysus; and their union is still remembered today in the constellation Corona, for he placed her crown in the sky after her death.

Here the ancient goddess showed herself through the Princess Ariadne in a new role, befitting the changing consciousness of the times. This mortal who had descended from the gods did not appear in a maternal role, instead she provided a life-sustaining thread to aid the growing human individuality as hero. But he needed to grow more mature before he would be worthy to be her partner. Meanwhile she slept, and she was still united with a god.

The Minoan-Mycenaean culture of Crete, with its echoes of the Great Mother goddess, disappeared into a dark age around 1200 BCE, and yet the influence of the Mother Goddess still lingered on the mainland of Greece even as powerful Zeus began his rule within the new patriarchal order. His great-grand-mother Gaia was still remembered as the Mother of all, through the stories of Homer and Hesiod.

Hymn to Gaia

Gaia
mother of all
foundation of all
the oldest one

I shall sing to Earth

She feeds everything
that is in the world

Whoever you are
whether you live upon her sacred ground
or whether you live along the paths of the sea
you that fly

it is she
who nourishes you
from her treasure-store[11]

~

Gaia was the goddess of Earth but was reduced to being the wife of Ouranos, God of Heaven, in spite of the fact that he had been brought forth as her first son. Though she was honored, it would be Zeus, with his thunder and ever-ready bolt of lightning, and no longer himself a creator god, who would become the ruling divinity for the Greeks. The people, too, were more warlike now, and dreams of conquest had supplanted peaceful coexistence.

Now there were many goddesses—sisters, mothers and daughters—each carrying a particular attribute of the once Great Goddess. Among the Olympians of Zeus's generation were Hera, the guardian of marriage; Hestia, goddess of the hearth; Demeter, goddess of the harvest; and Aphrodite, goddess of beauty and love. Fiery Zeus became the Great Father, and by marrying different goddesses and fathering others he could increasingly claim their former authority as his own.

Hera was an older sister to Zeus and became his wife, a role meant to reduce her lingering influence. Some of her children were powerful monsters, distorted images of the ancient Great Goddess, now destined to be slain by the emerging male heroes. Hera was known to be jealous, and understandably so with all that was being stripped from her as Zeus's power grew greater. She manifested a raging sense of injustice at the loss of her independence. The consciousness of the Greek people and their mythmakers was evolving. The gods and goddesses had more distinct personalities; their strivings and their mistakes were ever closer to the experiences of the people who worshipped them.

It was no surprise that Zeus's daughter Athena, the powerful goddess of war, was born—through cunning trickery—not of a mother, but from the head of Zeus. Warrior that she was, in her way she was also still a goddess of wisdom, reflecting for the Greeks a kind of balance between the wild expression of immediate impulse and a possibility of restraint, careful planning, and control. In Aeschylus' *Oresteia,* it is Athena who casts the final vote in favor of Orestes, who was being tried for the once unimaginable crime of murdering his mother. A final death knoll to the earlier times of matriarchal authority sounds in Athena's closing words at the trial: "There is no mother anywhere who gave me birth, / and, but for marriage, I am always for the male / with all my heart, and strongly on my father's side."[12]

Like Inanna before her, Greek Demeter was the goddess of harvest, of grain, of the cultivated earth and of the changing seasons. She was mother to Persephone, the maiden, the seed of new life, who was abducted into the dark realm of death.

Once again, the story tells of capture by the force of darkness—here Hades, lord of the underworld—and then the long search of the mother for the lost loved one, for a now missing part of her wholeness. Like Isis, Demeter circles the land in grief, disguised at times as an old woman sitting by a well; and no crops would grow until even Zeus, despite his hand in all that had occurred, must bow to Demeter's anger and reveal what has happened to her daughter. Then Persephone can return to her mother, but not completely. Because Hades tricked her into eating a pomegranate seed, she was obliged to return to his realm for one third of the year. She could rise in spring like the new growth, only to go back to the underworld with the falling seeds. In the seasonal rhythms maiden and mother are as one, and the earth made fertile with ever renewing life and death.

The loss and the finding of Persephone were celebrated in the Eleusinian Mysteries, about which we moderns know very little. But they included celebration of a sacred marriage and the birth of a holy child. And in nature the heavenly rains would come again to the waiting earth, so that the grain as child could grow. As ever the mother watched over this process of regeneration.

Into the myths of Greece and later Rome came human or part human-part divine heroes doing battle with frightening monsters in order to advance in status and power. Many of these threatening figures appeared as female beings—for example Medusa with snakes for hair and her sister Gorgons; or the Sirens, Circe, Scylla and Charybdis, who were such dangerous obstacles in Homer's *Odyssey*, or the Sphinx with her challenging riddle for Oedipus. These were beings of ancient and unpredictable power now instilling fear in the evolving individualities embodied by the heroes. Masculine forces were awakening and advancing, and the lingering memory of the all-encompassing mother was now painted in ever more frightening ways. Her progeny, working with destructive might, must be contained while the heroes' growing capacities and importance were to be celebrated. Many of the heroes also married an Amazon queen to absorb and harness her still remaining feminine influence in the hearts of the people.

At a great distance from Greece, the Norse people also looked to a darkening image of feminine influence. Here, as in other parts of the world, the stories were part of an oral tradition for thousands of years before they were written down. In the Norse myths there is a mighty giantess named Angrboda, partner of the trickster Loki. She was known as a witch, and her three offspring were a daughter Hel and two sons who became the fierce Fenris Wolf and the Midgard Serpent. These monster offspring showed their powers in Ragnarök, in the destruction of the gods. In stories from around the world divine powers were receding from human consciousness, while on earth human individualities were growing stronger.

Yet there was another way, a new way that the divine mother being was finding honor in classical Greece, no longer as the Great Goddess but known, at last, by her true wisdom name. As the initiation rites of the ancient mystery centers were becoming ever more obscure and corrupted, the human intellect was maturing, and individuals began to think in quite new ways. In the emerging academies of Plato and later Aristotle, Sophia was sought and loved within the development of Philosophy, *Philo-Sophia*, love of wisdom. She was still turned to for inspiration although her living being became ever more abstracted.

Meanwhile, within the first millennium BCE there were other peoples who still felt Sophia's great wisdom influence, even as there were stronger forces trying to contain it. From around 800 BCE the Hebrew Patriarchs began to write down what would become the Old Testament, stories that centered on Yahweh as the one creator God, without divine parentage, siblings, or offspring. The Hebrew people were being led away from a lingering relationship to a divine mother toward a new, now monotheistic, and strongly male centered conception of the divine. Here was a patriarchal god with unlimited power, and his influence would also go on into Christianity and Islam. Both of these later religions would look to the Old Testament as divine revelation and to an all-powerful male god who became a model for an all-male priesthood, and even for the power of fathers and husbands over the women in their lives.

Although in the beginning of Genesis (1:27), God created Adam and Eve in his own image, male and female, by the second Genesis telling of creation (2:7) Adam was formed from the dust of the earth. Then Eve, yet another face of the divine mother, was further reduced by the almighty male God to creation from the rib of Adam (2:22). The lingering influence of the goddess would become more contained, and even her long-time companion the snake was transformed into a being of temptation and evil. Yet this much-diminished Eve still held within her being the deep knowing that the rib from which she was formed offered protection to the heart. And remembering her true roots, she dared to reach for the fruit of the Tree of Knowledge, to once again be as a god. But this was to be a story about the Fall, so she and Adam were cast out of the Garden of Eden. They took on "coats of skin"—like all our earthly bodies—as another act of containment. The once great mother of all life was destined to become an earthly woman, no longer the divine source of creation but now portrayed as the bringer of earthly death and carrying the sin of disobedience.

Yet, even still, from the fourth century BCE, Sophia as Wisdom, or *Chokhmah,* appeared in the Wisdom books of the Old Testament as a feminine counterpart to God. In Proverbs 8:23–31, she told of her existence from the beginning, before earthly creation and always with her attention on the human being:

> The Lord possessed me in the beginning of his way, before his works of old.
> I was set up from everlasting, from the beginning, or ever the earth was.
> When there were no depths, I was brought forth: when there were no mountains abounding with water.
> Before the mountains were settled, before the hills was I brought forth:

> While as yet he had not made the earth, nor the fields, nor the highest part of the dust of the world.
> When he prepared the heavens, I was there: When he set a compass upon the face of the depth:
> When he established the clouds above: when he strengthened the fountains of the deep:
> When he gave to the sea his decree, that the waters should not pass his commandment: when he appointed the foundations of the earth,
> Then I was by him, as one brought up with him, and I was daily his delight, rejoicing always before him,
> Rejoicing in the habitable part of his earth, and my lights were with the sons of men.

Surely it was words like these that inspired Michelangelo some two thousand years later to paint, on the ceiling of the Sistine Chapel, the mysterious woman sitting by God's side at the creation of Adam.

> If "the god" initiates humanity into duality and the laws of time, then "the goddess" redeems that vision by releasing the mind from identification with mortality and reuniting it with the universal inexhaustible life out of which all particular lives come and go. In the metaphor that is mythology, this is the sacred marriage...immortality and wisdom can, finally, be offered together. (Anne Baring and Jules Cashford)[13]

A mighty change was coming to the world. A divine being was preparing to incarnate into a human body. This would bring a new unfolding of the ancient theme of mother and child. A very special mother was needed for this to happen—a great soul who could bring this spirit to birth, a Great Mother whose love would cradle this special one to earth and bear his mighty and free deed of sacrifice for the ongoing human story. This mother was seen as virginal—meaning a being complete within herself. Of course, there was also a father. Why else would the Gospels take so seriously the child's ancestry—in the case of Matthew, back to Father Abraham, and in Luke back to Adam? And what are we to make of these different lines of heredity? Could there have been two babies, two Mothers? Deep mysteries lie within these Gospel stories.

We hear of Jesus of Nazareth becoming a carpenter, growing into a man of unparalleled wisdom. By the age of thirty, he was suffering in his soul from how people misunderstood the sacred Hebrew teachings, he was pained by the decadence of the old mysteries, and troubled by the spiritual seclusion of the Essenes who in the purity of their strivings pushed evil outside their own gates and thereby into the lives of others. One day he was wandering alone, heavy at heart, when he met his Mother, and he was able to unburden these sorrows to her listening heart. This conversation was for him a katharsis. His Mother's deep bearing soul could manifest the wisdom of the Virgin Sophia; and through their encounter, Jesus could go on to the river Jordan to be baptized by John, to receive the Christ Being into his infinitely prepared soul.[14]

For all the devotion that the being of Mary has engendered in Christians throughout the last 2,000 years, and for all the many titles she was given by the Catholic Church—Blessed Virgin Mary, Mother of God, Gate of Heaven, Star of the Sea, Our Lady of Sorrows, Mother Most Pure, to name but a few—it was only within esoteric circles that she was recognized as a new, evolving, and human manifestation of the ancient Mother Goddess. Through all these years there were, thankfully, artists who could see her greater mystery and show her with the child on her lap as on a throne, surrounding her with the plants and animals that had always been part of her world—most especially the dove, the lily, and the rose. They also painted and sculpted her veiled, and often with the open book of wisdom on her lap or in the eager hands of the child.

And there were artists who also showed her with the child on her lap, but with still more—sometimes she herself was sitting on another's lap—a Mother of another dimension. Some referred to this holding mother as St Anne, Mary's mother, but to see such images is to know that a greater mystery is being revealed. The mother holding her own grown child belongs to the majesty of the Great Mother, echoing back to Neolithic times and beyond. Here is Sophia, the Wisdom of the World, veiled yet enveloping the wholeness of life.

In the early centuries after the time of Christ, the Gnostics remembered Sophia as an embodiment of Wisdom, as the partner to the male godhead from the beginning, as the womb of creation. And they were persecuted by the evolving Roman church until finally completely repressed under the edicts of Emperor Constantine in the 4th century. But truth will try to come again to human consciousness, and so in 1945, fifty-two Gnostic texts were found buried in upper Egypt. The broad and varied background of Gnosticism comes through in these Egyptian, Jewish and Greek texts now known as the Nag Hammadi

Library. Here the goddess tradition still lived in the story of the Great Mother Sophia.

One Gnostic text clearly echoes earlier images of the Great Mother that had sounded from Mesopotamian temple incantations through to the Old Testament Wisdom books. Here are but a few lines of what Wisdom—filled as she has always been with the paradox of wholeness—had to say in this verse known as *The Thunder, Perfect Mind*:

Look upon me, you who reflect upon me,
and you hearers, hear me,
You who are waiting for me, take me to
yourselves.

....

For I am the first and the last,
I am the honored one and the scorned one,
I am the whore and the holy one.
I am the wife and the virgin.
I am the (mother) and the daughter.
I am the members of my mother.

I am the barren one
and many are her sons.
I am she whose wedding is great,
and I have not taken a husband.
I am the midwife and she who does not bear.
I am the solace of my labor pains.
I am the bride and the bridegroom,
and it is my husband who begot me.

I am the mother of my father
and the sister of my husband,
and he is my offspring.

....

I am the one who has been hated everywhere
and who has been loved everywhere.
I am the one whom they call Life,
and you have called Death.
I am the one whom they call Law,
and you have called Lawlessness.
I am the one whom you have pursued,
and I am the one whom you have seized.
I am the one whom you have scattered,
and you have gathered me together...[15]

Among the myths related in the Gnostic texts, and buried away for more than 1,500 years, is one with strong echoes of Demeter and Persephone, once again presenting the human soul as the daughter of the Great Mother, both now bearing the name Sophia. Here, too, was a picture of a fall, recorded 1,000 years after the description of the Fall in the Old Testament—a devastating falling away of human consciousness from its source:

> Sophia appears as the primal Virgin Mother, consort of the Father God, and as the power through whom the creative source of life brings itself into being, the womb that generates all worlds and levels of being as her child. Like Egyptian Maat

> and Hokhmah in the Old Testament, she personifies Wisdom. Like Inanna, Hokhmah and the Shekhinah of later Kabbalistic mythology, she personifies Light. The mother Sophia gave birth to a daughter, the image of herself, who lost contact with her heavenly origin, and in her distress and sorrow brought the earth into being, and became entangled and lost in the chaotic realm of darkness that lay beneath the realm of light: a darkness or underworld that was identified with the earth sphere whose gates were guarded by fearsome planetary spirits, the archons. A curtain or barrier came between the worlds of light and darkness, making it impossible for the daughter Sophia to return to her parents. She was condemned to wander in this dark labyrinth, "endlessly searching, lamenting, suffering, repenting, laboring her passion into matter, her yearning into soul."... Like Persephone, the soul cries out in her distress to her Mother and Father in the transcendent world...the Virgin Mother Sophia, in response to her daughter's call, sends her son to rescue his sister. Her son is Christ, the embodiment of her Light and Wisdom, who descends into the darkness of his parent's furthest creation to awaken his sister to remembrance of her true nature.[16]

For the Gnostics, divine light was not to be found through belief or adherence to the authority of religious doctrine but rather through individual insight, as an inner experience. The soul on earth was not doomed by original sin; she was captivated by the entangling forces of earth until freed through awakening insight. As Sophia, the awakening soul would know of her indwelling spirit, made manifest by Christ. Gnostic ritual celebrated a sacred marriage between soul and spirit, but this very idea defied the emerging doctrine and power of the Roman Church. Such thoughts were declared heresy, and the many expressions of Gnosticism in the buried Nag Hammadi texts had to wait to be unearthed until there were eyes and ears able to penetrate further into these mysteries.

The stories of Mary the Mother and of Jesus Christ have been told for 2,000 years, and the future may still allow deepening dimensions of their great mystery to be known. She was there with her care at the birth of he who would offer his body to the universal spirit of love. She was with him during the three years he lived as a divine being in a human body, and at the cross she could trust in the resurrection to come. She was centrally there with the disciples around her at the Whitsun event. Many twists and turns have worked to distort the deep significance of that turning point in time. But as the universal spirit of humanity, her son is with us still, and connected, as she is as well, to our ongoing earth story, serving people of any faith or no faith, whether we know it or not. "It is not the

Christ we lack, but the knowledge and wisdom of the Christ, The Sophia of the Christ..."[17]

One extraordinary woman living in the 12th century did know Sophia as the being of Wisdom, referring to Her also as Sapientia and Caritas. Hildegard of Bingen was a spiritual leader and healer, a nun and an advisor to Popes, and the visionary author of several books, such as *Scrivias (Know the Ways)* and many hymns to Sophia. For her, Sophia was the connecting reality encompassing the divine world and humanity on earth. She unified the creator and the created world. "She is where God stoops to humanity and humanity aspires to God."[18] Hildegard perceived divine manifestation through Sophia; it was she who had made creation possible.

To Sophia

You soar, sustain, and animate,
climb, dive, and sing
Your way through this world,
giving life to every beating
heart.

You never end.
You keep circling, crossing over us
on three wings—
one speeds through heaven,
one holds the earth together
with a kiss as light as dew,

and one whooshes over, under,
and through our lives.
We praise You, Wisdom!
—Hildegard of Bingen

Threads of what the Gnostics knew continued to weave underground throughout later centuries, finding important moments of expression during the Middle Ages and into the early Renaissance—from the 11th to the 15th centuries. For example, the Cathars in France and northern Spain found inspiration in the Holy Spirit as Sophia. They sought to awaken their souls to their own indwelling divine nature, seen as the guiding spirit of Christ. This level of spiritual independence was deemed heretical by the Catholic Church of the time, and the Cathars were eventually destroyed by the Papal Crusade of 1209.

Throughout the Christian world devotion to Mother Mary grew during these years, an echo of the reverence offered the goddess for thousands of years. She was venerated by the people, more than by the established church, which struggled to contain her influence. She offered comfort and mercy through dark times and was experienced as a mediator between earth and heaven, between what was considered human and what divine. The sense of unity with the wholeness of the divine world became more fragmented as individual consciousness grew stronger. Within the practices of the Church, Mary was celebrated for her purity of soul and gentle motherhood even as her Great Mother spirit was gradually diminished. Still the troubadours sang her praises and around the world hundreds of churches were dedicated to her; in France alone over eighty cathedrals were built in honor of Notre Dame.

Shrines to the Black Virgin were also revered throughout Europe during the Middle Ages. Sometimes ancient goddess sites were rededicated to Mary, and Christian churches or cathedrals built on long-sacred ground. Early representations of the Black Madonna may have been statues of the earlier goddess, long hidden but now unearthed, or also ancient "pagan" images brought back from the Crusades by the Templars. These were re-envisioned as Mary, re-imaginings that allowed a continued celebration of important aspects of the pre-Christian Great Mother still longed for by questing souls. In contrast to the devotion to Mary within the church, as the pious mother and a comfort to the soul, the statues of the Black Virgin offered the many pilgrims who flocked to her sites a different kind of experience. Here the son was seated on her lap as on a throne; reverence for her was like an encounter with the Gnostic mother Sophia, Wisdom Herself. The Catholic Church did not support but could not eliminate this greatness. Like her son, She existed for all humanity, not only for those adhering strictly to any particular doctrine.

Chartres Cathedral is an example of the importance of Mary/Sophia for the people of the Middle Ages, and in fact up until today. There the Black Madonna is relegated to the Crypt, and the labyrinth that is inscribed into the floor as an echo of ancient Crete is often covered with chairs. But visitors who come in pilgrimage to the Great Mother still find her throughout the mighty cathedral—in the stained-glass windows with her regal child on her lap, in the many sculptures adorning the building, and also as the inspiration behind the female figures of the seven Liberal Arts. These handmaids of Wisdom were central to the learning that took place within the School of Chartres.

Another example of Lady Wisdom's presence in the Middle Ages can be seen in the rise of the Jewish esoteric tradition of Kabbalah. On a foundation reaching back to the goddesses of the Bronze Age in Mesopotamia and Egypt, the image of the Shekinah brought a resurgence of feminine imagery into these mystical texts. She was the radiance of light at the source of the created world, identified with the Holy Spirit and immanent in the human soul. "The Shekinah was called Queen, Daughter and Bride of Yahweh, and was, by implication, the mother of all human souls.... Life, or creation, is conceived in the divine union between Yahweh and the Shekinah."[19] As in the Gnostic myth of Sophia, the Shekinah suffers exile, first through the expulsion of Adam and

Eve from the Garden of Eden, and then as part of the history of the Jewish people. She weeps and waits for the exile to end, for manifest creation to no longer be cut off from the divine. This feminine aspect of the deity was central to the esoteric thinking of Kabbalism, but it found no place within other, more known, streams of Judaism.

And yet another way Sophia gained new attention in the twelfth and thirteenth centuries was with the growth of Alchemy, which not surprisingly also had roots reaching back to Sumeria and Egypt. Always the quest for a transformation of the soul, and yet again a reaching for the thread weaving through nature toward a new understanding of the interrelationship of spirit and matter. Gnostic ideas resurfaced in the imagery of Alchemy, in the search for an "incorruptible substance underlying matter.... The alchemical marriage between sun and moon, king and queen, spirit and soul (including body), expressed the essential identity of spirit and nature, so healing the split that had developed in human consciousness between these two aspects of life."[20] In the alchemist's quest the guide and inspiration was Sophia-Sapientia, Wisdom herself.

There is no end to the ways the Great Lady Wisdom has been felt throughout the centuries. The threads leading to her inspiring and unifying presence may have been covered over, may have been stretched thin, but they have not been broken. She was always there for those who sought her, for those with the eyes to see. She inspired the search for the Grail, she accompanied Dante through *The Divine Comedy*, she was present in the rise of Sufism, the esoteric side of Islam. The greatest of the Renaissance artists portrayed her majesty, beauty and mystery for their time and ours and into the future. She spoke to the hearts of mystics such as Jakob Böhme, she appeared to the philosopher Vladimir Solovyov, inspiring a school of Russian Sophiology. She showed an aspect of herself in the many sightings of Mary in the nineteenth and twentieth centuries, appearing to those with a prayerful open heart, often even to children. In the development of Theosophy, and later Anthroposophy, she is not only there in the name, but she is seen as Mother and Wisdom and the creator of all. And her presence is central in fairy tales of many cultures—the godmother, the old spinning crone, the wise witch.

It is important—to us and certainly also to Her—to acknowledge that in this telling of her story, we have been following her presence in the development of western consciousness, and even within this so much has been left out. The Great Mother manifested all over the world, and myths from many lands tell of her wisdom and creative power, her offerings, her wanderings, and her eventual diminishment to male divinities. In China she was known as Kuan Yin (Guanyin), "She who hears the cries of the world," and was sometimes considered a bodhisattva; She was, and still is, the goddess of mercy, available to those caught in fear, despair or uncertainty. Also within Buddhism Tara has varied roles as a deity of compassion, and still as a Wisdom Goddess. Powerful Hindu goddesses are representatives of Shakti, the feminine source of power in the universe, and these beings are known to be both creative and destructive. In Africa, too, there is a prominent feminine presence of wisdom, for example with the Yoruba people of West Africa whose sacred text, Odu Ifa, recognizes the need for the ever-evolving wisdom of the Mothers in its calls for harmony and balance with all creation. Among Native Americans, Sky Woman was the creative mother goddess for the Iroquois, and Changing Woman helped the Navajo in their struggles between good and evil. For various indigenous peoples, the revered mother goddess—by many names, and still today often in the hearts of the people—is involved in creation, and transformation, balancing life and death, while encountering the jealousies of others. The origin stories of Aboriginal peoples everywhere have been told for long ages and continue to offer the people a connection to the mother with images of history and hope.

And yet in recent centuries the concept of a goddess has often been widely debased, or conversely sentimentalized. In many places the very idea of a divine world with divine beings is much in doubt. The individual is ever stronger; the authority of church or temple or mosque is much questioned or not sought at all. Natural science has pursued miraculous discoveries about space and time, about the human being and the natural world; this latter is no longer recognized as the goddess Natura. Contemporary science tries to stay within the confines of the calculable, what can be weighed and measured. Its conceptual reach often becomes abstract, and its materialism rejects the very idea of the working of spirit.

Nevertheless, there is much in movement in the world of the 21st century. Questions of injustice and of the degradation of the earth arise around us and within us, accompanied by new searches for a living relationship to spirit, and to the earth as a living being. Growing numbers of people begin to listen to their hearts, as these begin to speak. But the mighty Mother of the world still stands threatened, like she who was portrayed in the Book of Revelation (12:1–4):

> And there appeared a great wonder in heaven: a woman clothed with the sun, and the moon under her feet, and upon her head a crown of twelve stars: And she being with child cried, travailing in birth, and pained to be delivered. And there appeared another wonder in Heaven; and behold a great red dragon, having seven heads and ten horns, and seven crowns upon his heads...and the dragon stood before the woman

> which was ready to be delivered, for to devour her child as soon as it was born.

There is threat, and there is help. In Revelations the child is *caught up unto God*, the Mother waits in the wilderness while the Archangel Michael and his angels wage war in heaven and cast out the great dragon onto the earth. This is a picture, beyond any particular religious tradition, strangely prescient of the world we now inhabit. We are beset by many challenges—in the social order, the environment, the care of children, to name only a few—and still there is help waiting to work with us as we awaken to the real needs of the present and the future, as we struggle to lift the veil.

The story goes on, but now it is ever more in our hands to make room for and receive what the future may bring.

~

I am struggling with her story
She who was always there
her becoming so complex
not one thread to be followed
but the whole ancient yarn
with the shearer
and the sheep
the fields and the farm
the weathered air everywhere
all the knots and connections

I am wrestling
to untangle
my rational mind trying
to hear what the heart would tell
of then and now and tomorrow
When did it happen
Where did it happen
When and where and also how
is it happening
still

After an Interesting Talk

Code Name Sophia, he said
and I knew what he meant
but also that I would never
speak of you that way
You are no abstract call name
not an abstraction at all
but all around and real
My heart knows you are being
yourself with a timely name
this time now
waiting for our human step

3/29/14

Chapter 3

Of Veils and Unveiling

Though it is difficult to say who she is, wherever we turn, we see traces of her coming—as if tracking the fringes of her mantle as it brushed aside the tangled, sclerotic cobwebs of centuries of cerebration. As she draws near, much that was forgotten is reentering consciousness, not only as memory but also from the future, as possibility.

CHRISTOPHER BAMFORD, *Isis Mary Sophia*

Wisdom is the prerequisite for love; love is the result of wisdom that has been reborn in the "I."

RUDOLF STEINER

The story of the Wisdom of the World, so often identified as a divine feminine being and more specifically now as Sophia, continues to develop in the twenty-first century. Ever more people are trying to understand its deepening dimensions, its shifting focus, and its echoing call. As contemporary people we are living in these echoes; their resounding urgency touches many hearts today and would wake us up to our place in the story. We need to open inner eyes and listen with ever more perceptive hearts if we would connect with all that is around us as we seek a path toward a future that does not destroy the earth, or others, or ourselves.

The inscription above the invisible and sleeping statue of the New Isis/Sophia in the myth that is recounted in Chapter One says: *I am the Human Being. I am the Past, the Present and the Future. Every mortal should lift my veil.* Here is a task for our contemporary world, but what can this mean in each of our real lives? How are we to understand, and to take up this call to lift the veil? Perhaps before we can consciously engage in the work of lifting a veil to the spirit, we need to consider what is our actual lived experience of veils?

A veil separates a would-be knower from what could be known if the veil were not there. But it also signals that there is something there worthy of attention, something that we might miss noticing in the general onslaught of sense impressions. Think of the veil worn by many Muslim women. This veil is a protection, a shield keeping the veiled woman from being directly observed. But it also announces a valuable reality there, behind the veil, even if as viewer I am prohibited to penetrate this threshold to a deeper encounter. Recent world events make clear the difference between the wearing of a hijab, or head scarf as a kind of veil, when this is a woman's personal choice or when it is enforced by government or religious leaders. Protests have arisen in Iran to the obligation for all Iranian women to keep their heads covered. Many feel that the time is over for enforcements of this kind of veiling. The challenge today to lift the veil presents itself in many different guises.

During the recent Covid pandemic most people wore masks, and we experienced the tension between protection and the partial blockage of facial expressions—smiles, frowns, wonder, sadness—that had been a normal part of how we previously came to know others and also express ourselves. Many have spoken of the joy of finally removing these masks, of course in order to breathe more freely, but also for the fuller revelation of each other. We knew there was more behind the masks, and we missed what had become veiled.

Many years ago, my husband and I visited a nighttime street market in a small town in Turkey, and as we wandered through the many stalls of fabrics, pottery, rugs, and trinkets for tourists, we were beckoned into a hidden courtyard by a smiling young man and offered cups of tea at a small table under a tree. Our host and a few companions wanted to speak with us, without putting any pressure on us to buy anything. It was a beautiful evening and conversing with strangers under an open sky of bright stars seemed a perfect way to spend it. As I sat there, I observed many curtained off areas around the open central space, and I wondered what was behind those colorful hangings. One of our hosts saw me looking and asked if I would like a tour around. I was amazed to discover the rich life going on in the different sections: women chatting over cups of tea, children playing games or sleeping, craft projects spread out on long tables. All of this that had been veiled to me suddenly appeared vibrant and real, as indeed it had always been.

Thinking about this experience later I was reminded of a long favorite quote from Ralph Waldo Emerson: "Every wall is a door." I found myself extending the metaphor of veiled rooms to my searching to know more about the spirit. Although I might not yet be able to see into invisible spirit rooms, I felt—and had done so even as a child—that there was life and being beyond the threshold of my sense perception. I wanted to know more.

~

JOURNAL—4/13/1999

...And Isis is veiled. Not to be seen except by a new wakefulness. In ancient times through initiation. And now? Through attending. To what?—to what must lie beyond the veil. So imagination must be there, a sense for the possible, a feeling for the future—or maybe, too, a memory of the past—but the idea of something beyond. Something that calls through the veil: come find me, seek and ye shall find, open and all will be revealed.

How is the veil to be lifted? To be parted? To be pierced? Parcival could find his way through with the right question. Can a question lift the veil? Who are you?—and you tell me. What are you, veil? You hold "live" and "evil"—why just these letters? Is this only in English? How many things veil true life? How is evil a veil? When does the act of veiling become evil and when does it reveal what lives?

A veil is a constant question.

~

When I hear in the myth the call to lift the veil, I do not imagine a goddess of old sitting grandly behind a diaphanous veil. *Sophia* is a name for the wisdom of the world, and where the veil shifts or lifts even slightly, we come into contact with more that we can know. Of course, there is so much more that blocks a deepening wisdom than literal, material veils. We are often prevented from really experiencing another or an idea by prejudice—the pre-judgments based on gender, race, class, nationality, religion, education, or even simply what we have heard from someone else. Our own "rightness" and all we already know can block us from new insights. Beliefs and traditions can open us to spiritual experience, but they can also narrow our view. Criticism, cynicism, and fear shield us from really perceiving what is presenting itself to our consciousness. Busyness, distraction, anger, or an inability to forgive, all act as obstacles to deeper knowing. Sometimes these very human behaviors offer necessary protection, sometimes we let them live on in us beyond any usefulness.

~

JOURNAL—10/24/2004

I want to go deeper…to wake up more…to perceive more fully. I feel like it's time to take a step—the signs are everywhere for me—questions that arise from within or come from (others). Insights that feel half-way here—and then I let life distract me. I feel like I'm in a mist—caught in a valley of my own sloth, or is it fear.… I know it's time to move somehow, but it's as if I have to really get dull, empty, will-less before the new can begin. And I'm there.

~

There is also the virtual world, with all its enticements and the endless facts available at our fingertips. Answers before questions can act as a very thick veil to living knowledge. And a digital appearance of life is often full of illusion. One of the most egregious, to me, of these illusions is the first robot made to look like a human being—a classically pretty young white woman, of course—activated in 2016. She could make simple responses to apparently casual questions from a human interviewer, and she appeared to "learn" and exhibit human-like facial expressions. And what was her name? Not surprisingly, Sophia. Ostensibly this was to honor the wisdom that was now in human hands, but in fact it is a mockery of Wisdom's truth and living essence. Of course, another such mockery is the acronym ISIS, for the terrorist Islamic State. Both of these "namings" serve to diminish the historical grandeur and the current spiritual significance of the Isis/Sophia being; they trivialize or demonize, and so further veil the true concept, perhaps also blocking the recognition of felt experiences.

During the pandemic many of us began to have meetings on Zoom. When I first saw the grid of little boxes full of heads, I thought of the New Isis/Sophia myth and the cloned 'apparent offspring' of the goddess. With so many Zoom events it was easy to forget that behind those boxed faces were real people, each with a complex life, with worries, joys, sorrows, and hopes. I felt it was my work to consciously re-member this truth, both before and during these meetings—to let my attention restore living dimension to those on the screen, to honor a connection beyond the usefulness of meeting this way.

MIT professor and researcher Sherry Turkle has studied the human costs of our love of technology as screens and social media have become ever more dominant in our lives. In particular she has been interested in "empathy" and how it awakens in real relationships between people who are trying to be authentic. She sees this kind of unveiling of ourselves to each other as what is most needed for a living human future. In her memoir, *The Empathy Diaries*, she states:

> Screens not only distract us but encourage us to look to others for our sense of self. What is lost when this new circle draws us in? Attention to others. Attention to oneself. The capacity for solitude without stimulation—which is where the capacity for empathy is born.... On our screens we became eloquent but edited our thoughts. Face-to-face, when we stumbled and lost our words, we revealed ourselves most to one another. Online, we preached authenticity but practiced self-curation. We were constantly in touch yet lonelier than before.... Technology makes us forget what we know about life. As it confronts us with the question of what we most value about life.[21]

All through our lives we encounter veils, and they help us to discover more about who we are, what lives in nature, and for what we might keep striving. Watch toddlers who say "I'm hiding" by covering their eyes. As we find them with a smiling "peek-a-boo" they are learning more about their own being, they see through this self-created veil and begin differentiating themselves from an initial sense of oneness with the parent and the world. Or think of the curtains at the sides of so many Renaissance paintings. Why are they there if not to announce that something important is being revealed? And every morning, we open our eyes: we lift a veil to the physical reality of waking life. When we go to sleep, we move behind that veil and toward the possibility of awakening into another reality. Esoteric teachers of many traditions speak of this living spirit realm available to our true self in sleep, whether we remember any experience of this in waking life or not. The eyelid, the wrapping on a gift, the fog that covers the view of a world we know but for the moment cannot see—there are so many veils that teach us about anticipating, about waiting, about opening ourselves to more.

Witness
By Denise Levertov

Sometimes the mountain
is hidden from me in veils
of cloud, sometimes
I am hidden from the mountain
in veils of inattention, apathy, fatigue,
when I forget or refuse to go
down to the shore or a few yards
up the road, on a clear day,
to reconfirm
that witnessing presence.

~

There are so many ways to practice attention, to practice shifting a veil. Perhaps it starts with a well-known condition for inner development: learn to distinguish the essential from the non-essential,[22] penetrate through the details of what is being experienced in order not to miss what really matters. Then there is truly listening to what is shared with us, beyond easy judgments or the contest of intellectual repartee, but rather listening with opened senses and an open heart. Nature observation invites us to perceive the mystery of development through a looking that transcends mere identification, simplistic comparisons, usefulness, or even beauty. Or we can reflect on moments in our biography, letting a memory come into a vivid picture, seen from the outside, allowing it to resound and reveal clues beyond what may have fallen into an often-told anecdote; then we may see into a deeper meaning of an encounter, a turning point, a stumbling or a leap forward. And every evening we can look back on the day just lived, not to condemn or praise ourselves or others, not to get caught in should-have fantasies, but to practice objectively viewing our movement through the day—perhaps even in a backward direction to help us be more alert—and so attune ourselves to perceive destiny unfolding.

And what does any of this have to do with Sophia? She offers a name that works for me for the sense of an enveloping presence in my life that I see as deeper wisdom trying to enlighten my days, calling me to acknowledge the possibility, depth, and responsibility implicit in my everyday life. Without pretension, it feels as if both She and I have need of each other; but we must find our relationship in freedom. Her divine being, seeming to come ever closer into our human story, is a call to me from across the threshold; and my awakening to her, offers back an invitation, one tiny opening through the dense materialism of our age, for her to act with us.

Indeed, it seems that a new relationship to Sophia's ongoing story is appearing not only in individual consciousness but also in the broader world around us. Many people today begin to feel that something is happening. The edges of what can be known through the senses begin to blur, hinting of another reality beyond the boundaries of sense experience. Something is calling with ever greater urgency to awaken our responsibility to the earth, to each other, to our human future. Inspirations are there for those who are attending.

The goddess does not necessarily appear now in flowing veils of light. We live in a very conceptual age, and it seems appropriate that this wisdom being also now offers light and inspiration through concepts and ideas that appear and take root in our social order. I see an example of this in the way the idea of *inclusivity* swept through social discourse and policy in recent years. Of course, people have worked against discrimination of many kinds for many decades. But suddenly the word on everyone's lips was *inclusivity*; it invited new awareness and more attentive actions. In many settings there was a sense of urgency and possibility. The concept itself fired imaginations for social improvements in multiple ways.

I feel Sophia's whispers behind many contemporary efforts for social, ecological, and moral improvements.

She makes available new insights into the wisdom of the world in places where these are desperately needed. Can we humble our sense of human superiority, and awaken to yet unperceived secrets and cycles of nature? Can we participate with awakening attention and responsibility in an expanding cosmos of consciousness? For many decades I have been involved in developing what are called in the United States Biography and Social Art activities, and similar work is happening in many other places around the world.[23] This exploration of how universal laws of development are at work in an individual life serves not only the aim of greater self-knowledge, but through the many exercises shared in small groups, it also provides practice in awakening interest in others. It is a work of lifting the veil.

Another example of Sophia's influence is in the field of death care, in which it is possible to see an ever-growing attention to the threshold between life and death not as an absolute end to perceivable reality, but as a doorway of consciousness between realms of experience. I would say that this is coming through a new relationship to what is available from the wisdom of the world. Since the middle of the last century, more and more people are exploring beyond either their inherited ideas of heaven and hell or the materialistic atheism of our times. There are ever more discussions in popular culture about near-death experiences, as well as descriptions in esoteric literature about life after death, or before birth.

These often address the challenges of navigating between worlds. One recent example among many is Iris Paxino's *Bridges Between Life and Death*, which begins with these words:

> ...the deceased are not dead. What animated their body—their essence, their consciousness, their spirit—lives on in another form in a spiritual world interwoven with our earthly one. The departed have not ceased to exist, nor have we ceased to exist for them. They love and need us just as much as we love and need them.[24]

Connected to this opening to the threshold between life and death is the phenomenon of increasing numbers of people now considering reincarnation, not just as a learned belief but because of a growing inner feeling they have come to trust. This may play out in surprising "recognitons," such as an unexpected, and usually unarticulated, feeling of, "Oh hello again! I know you," on meeting someone. It might also come in the inner voice of, "Oh no, not you again!" Where does this sense of "again" come from? I am not suggesting pictures of earlier lives suddenly appear; rather something more like a faint echo, a whisper of unexpected familiarity. Or we might feel an unflagging necessity to pursue a particular interest, theme, or area of study to which we feel inexplicably drawn. What we do with these sorts of urgings may challenge our understanding of freedom in this life, but when we encounter them, they can feel embedded within an intention we seem to have been born with, perhaps even a felt compulsion, or a sense of destiny-laden responsibility.

Many people today live with an ambiguous relationship to the moral requirements of a healthy and supportive social order. By using the word "moral" this way, I am not speaking of outwardly imposed rules or a particular code of behavior. I truly believe the times for that—except perhaps in the careful raising of children—are over. But our future, the future of the earth and all her inhabitants, depends on individual moral development if we are not to destroy each other through self-centeredness, a distorted competitive drive, greed, and the machinations of power. I experience Sophia as an embracing presence, encouraging me to ever and again find my own integrity and moral bearings. The wisdom of what is needed, of what is right in any given situation is there to be perceived if I am attentive enough and honest enough. This does not come as a commandment, but as an opportunity for consciousness, and as an invitation for loving action. "Be the change you seek in the world," a statement derived from similar words said by Gandhi, has been folk wisdom sounding for several decades, and it is true. We will not make a better world—within ourselves, in our families and institutions, nor in the broader social order—with good ideas that we are not trying to embody day after day.

And of course, our world is all too full of darkness, suffering and much decidedly immoral behavior. If we speak of positive working spiritual beings, we need also to consider adversarial forces at work to stop human progress. I am very grateful to Rudolf Steiner for helping me to see that there is not a simple duality between good and evil. Rather there are different kinds of challenging forces active within all of us, and around us in society. Beings who would puff us up with self-importance, perhaps blinding us to the very real, contemporary needs on earth that require our human attention. And then also, beings who would turn us into well-functioning machines, binding the human spirit ever more to material reality. How do we, individually and collectively, find our way forward, balancing moment by moment the many pulls and pushes within and around us? How do we listen for guidance alive within the wisdom of the world and so find, ever and again, our own relationship to a living and loving moral center?[25]

The different religions of the world have long sought to guide their followers in how to live moral lives, but more and more cracks have appeared in the ways this traditional guidance has been delivered and in the narrowness of many outer behavior-based interpretations. Increasing numbers of people cannot find within the various places of worship an active and alive connection to spirit. The old dogmas are no longer enough. Many now seek a relationship to the spirit, but no longer through religion. This can be a lonely search, but it can also be a road to enlivening new forms of inspiration, connection, and community.

The twentieth century was filled with persecutions and horrific atrocities, and yet it also brought expanding efforts for civil rights of all kinds—religious, ethnic, national, racial and gender-based. It is not hard for me to picture a maternal wisdom embracing and defending an ever deeper and richer picture of human beings, human potential, and human community. Certainly, the development of psychology throughout the century was an important effort to lift the veil for a deeper understanding of the human psyche, the soul. Sometimes the journey of the human spirit within the soul's experiences was overlooked in the general matter-based emphasis of the times; and yet in many significant ways, psychology opened doors to ongoing explorations into the complexity of human life and relationships. In the 21st century, efforts toward social justice, psychological understanding, and a more living appreciation of our human differences have continued to evolve, as of course have regressive practices of racism, misogyny, nationalism, projected blame, and a fearful hatred of "the other."

The pandemic brought out the best and the worst in people, from daily expressions of kindness and care to shocking rudeness in stores, and sadly to deep partisan divisions in families and neighborhoods. For example, fierce judgments entered so easily into conversations about the virus, and about the vaccine. For me, the real enemy, the really dark force at work became ever clearer, and had very little to do with which side of this self-righteous battle one was on. Fear itself, whether of the virus or of the vaccine, was attacking people's souls, pulling them away from responsible consciousness, separating them from a living interest in others, feeding an alienating self-interest and a tragic judging of others. Of course, there were important individual, family, local and national decisions to be made—as there always are. These needed great individual and community responsibility, and mutual respect; but what showed up so often, accompanying the endemic fear, were severe critiques about the motives of others. The pandemic presented us with multi-leveled challenges about whom to trust, care for self and others, authority, and individual responsibility.

~

> What is this thing that has happened to us? It's a virus, yes. In and of itself it holds no moral brief. But it is definitely more than a virus....
>
> Whatever it is, coronavirus has made the mighty kneel and brought the world to a halt like nothing else could. Our minds are still racing back and forth, longing for a return to "normality," trying to stitch our future to our past and refusing to acknowledge the rupture. But the rupture exists. And in the midst of this terrible despair, it offers us a chance to rethink

> the doomsday machine we have built for ourselves. Nothing could be worse than a return to normality.
>
> Historically, pandemics have forced humans to break with the past and imagine their world anew. This one is no different. It is a portal, a gateway between one world and the next. We can choose to walk through it, dragging the carcasses of our prejudice and hatred, our avarice, our data banks and dead ideas, our dead rivers and smoky skies behind us. Or we can walk through lightly, with little luggage, ready to imagine another world. And ready to fight for it. (Arundhati Roy)[26]

~

Waking up to our collective sisterhood and brotherhood must happen individually. Yet exciting experiments in building community are growing all around us. Collaborative learning, work cooperatives, housing and land trusts, and CSA (community-supported agriculture) initiatives are but a few of the many activities being tried all over the world, if mainly on a small, local scale, with great devotion and imagination. More and more people are stepping out of traditional roles, family groupings, and even national identities to develop and practice new ways of strengthening more conscious connections with others.

People also begin to speak of the importance of community in quite new ways, not only as a humanly created place that could serve my personal well-being, but in recognition of a much greater inter-connectedness at work in the world. For example, what can we learn from the ways that trees communicate with and help each other? A novel like Richard Powers' *Overstory* perhaps won the 2019 Pulitzer Prize because it touches a growing sense that a forest is not made up of isolated, singular entities any more than our human society is. The science behind such a novel was presented in Suzanne Simard's *Finding the Mother Tree: Discovering the Wisdom of the Forest.* Through years of careful research, she has been able to show the mutual dependence and support that exist in a forest when human intervention and one-species planting for profit have not destroyed the living relationships in plant diversity.

Other contemporary researchers and thinkers are also expanding the boundaries of materialistic science. In this age of ecological emergency, there are an increasing number of thinkers who approach the natural world with humility and, beyond that, refuse to become caught in a false dichotomy between quantifiable natural science and more comprehensive indigenous or spiritual ways of looking at the earth. And so, we begin to have books like Robin Wall Kimmerer's best-selling *Braiding Sweetgrass: Indigenous Wisdom, Scientific Knowledge, and the Teachings of Plants,* which acknowledge the legitimacy and importance of both. The future seems to be asking us to address the ecological challenges that surround us by discovering new avenues of connection in nature and the cosmos that can enliven our vast technological know-how.

Another contemporary writer who addresses the reality of interconnectedness is Charles Eisenstein. In a recent online essay, he looks at how the shared stories—the mythology—of a culture or a time period inform our lives and our actions. Commonly held assumptions, weaving through varying degrees of consciousness, determine our understandings of the world around us and of our own human nature. He suggests that for a very long time we have been informed by the "Story of Separation," but that a new narrative, which he calls the "Story of Interbeing," is now beginning to resound. He presents a long list of self-defining insights and actions in the contrasting voices of both the old story and the new story, and then he closes his essay with these words:

> You can see that neither of these two stories is a disconnected list of things we like or things we don't like. Each item coheres with all the others. This explains the natural alliance that someone working to end punishment-based "justice" may feel with someone working to develop holistic beekeeping practices. What exactly is this movement of which so many of us feel a part? We are drawing from the same story, seeking the same story, sometimes acting from the same story. We

> are trying to translate it into relationships, politics, systems, gardens, parenting, work, education, technology, money, medicine, and religion. We may not always agree on what the story is. We may hold healthy resistance to uniformity of our stories, but that doesn't matter because ultimately we are not their creators. It is our stories that create us.[27]

And then the question that arises for me is: Who is whispering these new stories into our ears, our hearts, our deeds?

It seems to me that in many different ways Sophia is trying to enter our consciousness, trying to offer us more of the wisdom of the world. Perhaps the experience of the pandemic, the hours at home, the loneliness away from offices and schools, families, and friends, gave people time to reflect on what really matters to them. Unless entrapped by forces of division and enmity, ever more people are exploring things like more living community, relational decency, inclusivity, resilience for self and others, meaningful work, or social justice. And many begin to recognize these activities as practice in the cultivation of love.

An excerpt from a SteinerBooks' "Sunday Letter" by John Scott Legg:

> In his lectures on the Gospel of John, among other places, Rudolf Steiner pointed to the ubiquity of wisdom in our outer, earthly world. Wherever in

the great world of nature one turns, and the deeper one goes, there is wisdom: the inner workings of grand ecosystems; the mutuality and abundance of life in oceans, forests, grasslands, and even deserts; the digestive systems of cows and owls; the miracle of water; the movement of celestial bodies; dark and light; day and night; in each and every cell and star and planet, we find wisdom.

We dwell in a cosmos of wisdom, and yet this wisdom is an inheritance, born of the deeds of the past. Like all else, it must die and be reborn—as the cosmos of love.

"Divine creation is not simply a repetition of something already existing. Each planetary existence had a very definite mission. The mission of our Earth is the cultivation of the principle of love to its highest degree by those beings who are evolving upon it. When the Earth has reached the end of its evolution, love should permeate it through and through." (Rudolf Steiner, *The Gospel of St. John*, May 20, 1908)

Thoughts such as this are not given wide exposure in the discourse of our time, and never could they be forced upon anyone. But freely found, tested, and put to use, they can open doors of insight and action, both now and in the future. (Oct. 2022)

It's difficult to speak of love without falling into sentimentality. But real love—not only as a feeling, but as a verb, as activity—is the fruit of freely attending, and finding a way to offer what is needed. Wisdom and love—we long for both without necessarily recognizing how they belong together, how they relate to each other. But we need to know, to hold a space of bearing in our heart's consciousness, if love is to be born. A mighty archetype of this can be seen in the story of the conversation between Jesus and his Mother before the Baptism. Her deep listening helped to create space for the Christ Being to come to earth. This Christ Being descended from the realm of the Sun to the Earth to inhabit the profoundly prepared body and soul of Jesus of Nazareth, becoming a representative for, and of, all humanity, a divine being so much greater and more inclusive than any one religious tradition has been able to express.[28]

In a lecture referred to in chapter 1, *The Search for the New Isis, Divine Sophia,* Rudolf Steiner spoke of the ways the Isis/Sophia being had been wrenched away from human consciousness in earlier centuries, and especially during the rise of materialism in the nineteenth century—he even used the word *killed*—and how it is now our task to re-awaken to her all-bearing wisdom presence. He spoke of how the Christ Being, since the crucifixion and resurrection, is ongoingly connected to the earth and to our human story—to all humanity and not only as articulated within traditional Christianity—but that we have lost the capacity to know this enduring truth, to recognize this being of Love. As Steiner stated, "It is not the Christ we lack, but the knowledge and wisdom of the Christ, The Sophia of the Christ..."[29]

> ...knowing Sophia is possible because of the influence of Sophia. This knowledge of Sophia can lead in turn to insights on other topics. It is parallel to and in contrast to a materialistic cycle: a person's conviction that all is matter is confirmed by the apparent inaccessibility of spirit. Only spiritual thinking can access Sophia—and only if one looks in her direction and strives to think as a spiritual being and by a spiritual method. A person is not likely to find what they are not seeking, and especially will not find what they believe does not exist. It is the mission of Anthroposophia to collaborate with spiritually striving souls in order to resist the dominant materialist world view and to complement and balance it by knowledge of spiritual beings. (Robert McDermott)[30]

~

JOURNAL – 1995

This poem by Judith Wright was given to me by a student here in Australia, as I wander on my sabbatical. It's humbling. And yet, what else is there?

What would I wish to be?
I wish to be wise.
From the swamps of fear and greed
free me and let me rise.
There was a poet once
spoke clear as a well-cast bell.
Rumi his name; his voice
rings perfect still.
O could I make one verse but half so well!

What do I wish to do?
I wish to love:
that verb at whose source all verbs
take fire and learn to move.
Yes, could I rightly love,
all action, all event,
would from my nature spring
true as creation meant.
Love takes no pains with words
but is most eloquent.

To love, and to be wise?
Down, fool, and lower your eyes.

~

Many people who have had an interest in Rudolf Steiner's work have lived with questions about the nature of the "Sophia" in the name Anthroposophia, which is how he named the movement developing from his ideas. The human being coming toward

Divine Wisdom, or perhaps Divine Wisdom coming toward the human being? Steiner himself said this:

> The term *Anthroposophy* should really be understood as synonymous with "Sophia," meaning the content of consciousness, the soul attitude and experience that make a person a full-fledged human being. The right interpretation of *Anthroposophy* is not "the wisdom of the human being," but rather "the consciousness of one's humanity."[31]

In 2019 a group of people interested in Anthroposophy from around the United States began to meet on Zoom to explore Sophia through our own experiences and questions. We were drawn toward this work through many doorways, such as myth, feminism, philosophy, education, death care, star wisdom, healing, esoteric studies, and contemporary life itself. The 2021 winter-spring issue of the journal published by the Anthroposophical Society in America, *Being Human*, contained a collection of one-paragraph reflections by several members of the group. This was called "A Sophia Mosaic."[32] Here are just a few sentences from those reflections:

> Sophia is living process.... If Sophia were likened to a story or a poem, she would be the space between the words that allows meaning to find its way to human hearts and minds.... Awakening to Sophia is to participate in a conversation that has no beginning or

end, it is a beautiful movement between being heard and listening deeply, as revelation reveals revelation. (Angela Foster)

...I feel Sophia when I stand at the river's edge and witness the vast array of colored leaves on a fall day.... I sense her deeply in the interlude of dusk and rising of morning light when I feel the quiet shifting of light to dark, and dark to light. She awakens in me the true understanding of life into death and death into rebirth. (Michele Mariscal)

As the contours of my soul/spiritual life ever so gently gain in definition, I've begun to perceive Sophia as a prominent presence gracing my inner altar. I experience this intimate sanctuary as an architecture constructed of space rather than filled form, as mood rather than material. Yet the felt experience is far from abstract or immaterial! (Jordan Walker)

There is an embrace waiting. Waiting when I lay down my self, when I lay down my mind. A vessel holding equally what it also can pour. There is a hand on one's back, a cloak around the shoulders, a wind running fingers through the hair.... Each time we encounter the unknown there is trepidation, then holy suspension, and then the opening of a mysterious new door.... When I

> brace myself, what am I expecting? When I surrender, what can I find? (Tess Parker)

> ...It is Sophia: She who lives into the humblest regions of my humanity, my life and work, consecrating every conscious deed despite all my unconsciousness. It is She who makes my life in community possible with the hope that Wisdom become Love, and Love become the healing force that would touch my confined world, and then even the whole world. (Carrie Schuchardt)

In December 1923, at the re-founding of the Anthroposophical Society in Dornach, Switzerland, Rudolf Steiner spoke the Foundation Stone Meditation. Each day during what is known as the Christmas Conference, he elaborated different sections or rhythms of this profound meditation. These rhythms bring different parts of the meditation together, suggesting layers of significance. Working with these rhythms invites ever renewing life forces into our meditative activity. As the words and the rhythms resound within us, we can move beyond the boundaries of physical reality toward a perception of what is at work behind and within life itself: we can enter the etheric realm, the realm of living formative forces.

Rudolf Steiner said that he was laying this Foundation Stone into the hearts of his listeners, for the founding of a home for Anthroposophia on earth. Can we imagine

Anthroposophia as a being, as an aspect of Heavenly Sophia, now coming into our human experience on our evolving earth? Already in 1913, Steiner had this to say:

> What we receive through anthroposophy is our very own being. This once floated toward us in the form of a celestial goddess with whom we were able to enter into relationship. This divine being lived on as Sophia and Philosophia, and now we can once again bring her out of ourselves and place her before us as the fruit of true anthroposophical self-knowledge.... It is the essence of anthroposophy that its own being consists of the being of the human, and its effectiveness, its reality, consists in that we receive from anthroposophy what we ourselves are and what we must place before ourselves, because we must practice self-knowledge.[33]

F. W. Zeylmans Van Emmichoven, who was mentioned in chapter 1, was present at the Christmas Conference. He is supposed to have said that after hearing the Foundation Stone Meditation, he felt he truly incarnated into his body for the first time. He later wrote that he experienced the Foundation Stone Meditation as a metamorphosis of the New Isis/Sophia Myth that Rudolf Steiner had told five years earlier, in 1918.[34] I have lived with this thought for many years and have come to feel its inspiring truth. It is one way, among many others, to approach this complex meditation.

In the myth the inscription over the invisible sleeping figure of the New Isis/Sophia statue reads: *I am the Human Being. I am the Past, the Present, and the Future. Every mortal should lift my veil.* The Foundation Stone Meditation begins with a mighty threefold call to the Human Soul. In ancient Mystery Schools, the pupil was exhorted to "Know Thyself." Here in the first three panels of the meditation, the human being, having been called to awaken, is offered mighty imaginations of our archetypal human becoming. We are informed about the three realms in which we live: *You live within the limbs; You live within the beat of heart and lung; You live within the resting head.*[35] Each of these realms of human life is then elaborated in terms of its respective relationship to space, time, or eternity. These mantric words are telling us who we are in our deepest spiritual sense, and also what the inscription in the myth is referring to when stating, *I am the Human Being.*

Then in each of the panels a practice is elaborated. This is what we are to do if we would come to know who we truly are, if we are to consciously cross the threshold to a perception of spirit realms, if we are to lift the veil: *Practice spirit-recalling / In depths of soul; Practice spirit-sensing / In balance of the soul; Practice spirit-beholding / In stillness of thought.* The inscription in the myth says, *I am the Past, the Present, and the Future*; and these practices take us into these different realms: the first into the past and into the realm of the *wielding / World-Creator-Being*;

the second into the *surging deeds / Of World-evolving* in the present moment; and the third to *where the gods' eternal aims / Bestow the light of cosmic being* from the future.

The practice of these different exercises can take us in many directions. Why do we practice anything in life—an art, a discipline, a skill? We want to make it such a part of ourselves that we can play music from our heart because the notes and rhythms live within us; so that we can offer our artistic capacities to the painting that waits to come onto the canvas; so that the character who would walk onto the stage can use our hours of learning lines and blocking scenes; so we can enliven dry information with the warmth of living thinking. Practice allows us to freely offer our developing self to a desired activity. Through these spirit practices of the Foundation Stone, we are nurturing new organs of perception with which to lift the veil to a deeper spirit knowing.

Spirit-recalling, or remembering, brings our attention to the world of creative forces, to all that is available to us from the past—to what lives in our will as karmic intention, and also in the whole created world, and in the evolution of consciousness throughout history. As individuals we carry our destiny, our unconscious will in our limbs and muscles as they take us where we need to be. How can we practice spirit-recalling? We can attempt a retrospective look at what lives in the past: a daily review of our actions, biography exercises that awaken karmic intention, research and study into the created world of nature or history, and also a view into the becoming of the cosmos. Practicing spirit recalling awakens gratitude for all we have been offered from what is referred to as the Father ground of existence.

The practice of *Spirit-sensing*, or spirit mindfulness, calls for *balance of the soul* as we attend to the *rhythms of time*. We live within so many rhythms of ongoing transformation: breathing, heartbeat, sleeping and waking, life and death, the seasons, also inner and outer, expansion and contraction. Do we have an awareness of the present moment within the stream of time, within the ongoing world becoming? In the beginning of the myth the New Isis/Sophia being thought that she loved her visitor, and she thought that he was the father of her offspring, even as she was unable to understand the true nature of this offspring. In not being able to sense the spirit truth of her situation, she dragged her offspring through the world until it fell to pieces. Here in the Foundation Stone meditation, we are challenged to practice a living presence of heart and mind, a true sensing within ongoing transformations, within *the surging deeds / Of world-evolving*. Here we need to find our own balance, to feel centered in ourselves, with reverence for what we are encountering. Rudolf Steiner's Six Exercises, as well as the Eightfold Path, can help us awaken living perception within the weaving of each present moment.[36]

In practicing *Spirit-beholding*, or envisioning, we would make space for an experience of *world thoughts*. This takes us beyond the past or the present and into the timelessness of *the gods' eternal aims*. We would behold in the stillness of the resting head a bestowal of *the light of cosmic being / On your own I*. This is a listening into spirit truth. It is the practice of living thinking as elaborated in Steiner's *Intuitive Thinking as a Spiritual Path*, an exercising not for fixed answers, but toward true intuition, freely perceived moral intuition. The needs of what is coming toward us begin to speak. Rather than further activating our busy minds and all we already know, we are challenged in ourselves to become a living question, a quiet open heart. When the new Isis dimly follows what has happened to her offspring—the cloning into fourteen apparent offspring each bearing the false countenance of the New Typhon—she is aware that she is somehow responsible for what has happened, but she still lacks the ability to clearly intuit the truth.

The activity elaborated in each of the panels of the meditation creates the possibility to *truly live / In human world-all being*; to *truly feel / In human soul's creating*; and to *truly think / In human spirit depths*. How might we understand this use of *truly?* The work of the different practices is to develop objective organs of perception, through the purification of our soul or astral body. Rudolf Steiner spoke often of this task of our age—which he referred to as the age of the Consciousness Soul. In his cosmic evolutionary picture, this aspect of our soul is to be transformed in a future age into what he calls the Spirit Self. This latter is sometimes referred to in esoteric literature as the Virgin Sophia. In Steiner's words: "This cleansed, purified astral body, which bears within it at the moment of illumination none of the impure impressions of the physical world, but only the organs of perception of the spiritual world, is called in esoteric Christianity 'the pure, chaste, wise Virgin Sophia.'"[37]

The first part of each of the three panels of the meditation sounds a call to us to wake up to our true nature as beings of body, soul, and spirit. So much else calls to us in our everyday lives and works to form us in more matter-bound ways. We are surrounded by images and temptations of apparent human requirements: money, success, power, the right clothes and other objects of pleasure or status. We can easily become lost in material characterizations of what it means to be a human being. The Foundation Stone speaks to a different reality of our being and calls us to deeper attending. The call is to us as individuals, but within a world of human brotherhood and sisterhood, and this within a world of cosmic activity where our *own "I"/Comes into being/In the "I" of God;* and where we will *unite your own "I"/With the "I" of the World;* and *Where the gods' eternal aims/ Bestow the light of cosmic being/On your own "I" / For free and active willing.* The meditation is speaking to an essential and "true" spirit aspect of our individual being and becoming, even as it is preparing the ground for a new community where individual freedom is paramount.

After the first part of each of the three panels there is a pause, a break in the text, and the veil begins to shift; a threshold is crossed, revealing the working of spirit behind the outer phenomena of our human reality. Could we see this as an evolving transformation of the two crowns worn awkwardly by the awakening New Isis/Sophia—the cow horns of her ancient Egyptian clairvoyance and the paper crown full of all the scientific data of the present age? In the myth and often in our lives, these different ways of knowing—each valid on its own terms—sit next to each other with little integration. But they are both part of a greater whole, which we are now challenged to embrace in a new way as we move into the future.

Having touched what it is to "truly" live, feel, and think, the second part of each panel begins with the word *For*. This is not a causal explanation for the intellect, but an invitation into the background of all that has come in the first part of the three panels, in these layered pictures of who we are. We enter first into the realm where the *Father-Spirit of the heights holds sway,* then we come to where the *Christ-will encircling us holds sway,* and last, we are led to where the *Spirits' world-thoughts hold sway.* We find ourselves now with the Trinity, first the Father—*In depths of worlds begetting life;* then in the realm of the Son—*In world rhythms, bestowing grace upon souls;* and finally in the world of Spirit—*In cosmic being, imploring light.*

Through the practices of the "I" in the beginning sections, we now approach the macrocosm, the realms of spiritual hierarchies, here referred to as *Spirits of Strength* (Seraphim, Cherubim, Thrones); *Spirits of Light* (Kyriotetes, Dynamis, Exusiai); and *Spirits of Soul* (Archai, Archangeloi, Angeloi). Sounding forth from these hierarchies comes a renewal of important Rosicrucian words from earlier times. First, what rings forth from out of the heights is echoed in the depths with words of creation: *Out of the Godhead we are born.* Then in the second panel, what is enkindled in the east takes on form in the west, and in a mood of love are spoken the words: *In Christ death becomes life.* In the third panel we come closer in our human longing with the plea that what is entreated or prayed in the depths might be heard in the heights, and the answer comes: *In the spirit's cosmic thoughts the soul awakens.* Here in this second part of the meditation, we are touching the mysteries of birth, death and resurrection, and spirit awakening.

Working with the totality of the three panels we can try to live into the fullness of what we are as human spirit beings, into a fulfillment of what is sounded in the threefold call to the Human Soul. We are lifting the veil. Divine Wisdom herself is resurrected within us through our practice and our awakening. What Steiner referred to as having been "killed" by our modern intellect begins to come alive in us in ways appropriate to the times in which we live.

At the end of each of the three panels, after a pause each time, there sounds a mysterious echo of the place in the myth where the New Isis/Sophia came, at last, to a living understanding of the true nature of her offspring. This was after it had been falsely cloned into the fourteen apparent offspring bearing the countenance of the New Typhon—the adversarial force of our age, now known to some by the name Ahriman. It was through the help of elemental spirits of nature that the New Isis/Sophia was able to recognize what had happened to her offspring, and now to "truly" experience it. She knew that she had somehow been involved in all that had transpired; but now, with a living capacity of perception into the etheric world of the elementals or nature spirits—into the world of formative life forces—her offspring was restored to her in its true form. In the Foundation Stone meditation, we hear repeated three times, after each of the panels: *This is heard by the spirits of the elements / In east, west, north, south: / May human beings hear it!* All that was sounded in the three panels about the human archetype, about the past, the present, and the future, about the Trinity and the offerings of the Hierarchies has been heard by the spirits of the elements. *May*—it is within our individual freedom—we human beings hear these cosmic truths.

And if we do—and this is not once and for all, but ever and again—then we can come to understand, as the New Isis/Sophia eventually did, the true meaning of the Logos as described in the Gospel of John. In the fourth panel of the meditation, we now hear the story of what occurred *At the turning point of time.* The true meaning of the Mystery of Golgotha, of the life and death and resurrection of the Christ Being begins to resound in our hearts. Where darkness had reigned, *The spirit-light of the world/Entered the stream of earth existence,* with a light that warms simple shepherds' hearts and enlightens the wise heads of kings. And in the myth the cow horns take hold of the paper crown, and the one true golden crown of the New Isis/Sophia is revealed.

In the second and final part of the fourth panel [page 109], the deed of founding a home on earth for Anthroposophia—a human face of Divine Wisdom in our times—is sounded as a prayer to *Light divine,* to Christ as a being of the Sun, now interwoven with our human earthly story. The plea is to *Warm/Our hearts;/Enlighten/Our heads;/That good may become.* As the center piece of the conference to renew the work of the Anthroposophical Society, Rudolf Steiner referred to the entire meditation as a foundation stone of love being placed in human hearts in order to create a place for Anthroposophia in our souls, in the Human Soul. Our hearts, our heads and our focused will are all needed for this soul reception. And these final words of prayer speak to *our* human task—not only as individuals, but as true sisters and brothers—that what is founded may resonate with the bounty of the Heavenly Sophia's earth loving words, and nurture new community in the divine light of which they speak.

> The being Anthroposophia seeks in our time to lead humanity to a mastery of that wholly new inner faculty that Rudolf Steiner calls conscious...clairvoyance and that has its foundation in the transformation of the consciousness soul into the imaginative soul. (Sergei O. Prokofieff)[38]

At the founding for an earthly home for Anthroposophia, Divine Wisdom herself was there, telling us who we are and calling forth our ongoing becoming. With the Foundation Stone meditation, we are invited to lift the veil to greater spirit knowing. As we contemplate this articulation of the human archetype, the spiritual imagination out of which we are evolving, we also meet the challenge to make real the possibility of human freedom.

There are, of course, many other ways and venues in which Sophia is speaking today; it feels increasingly urgent to me that in many different ways, we now listen with devoted attention and intention to her calling.

In closing, I want to bring these considerations back to our daily lives and to the many challenges we face in our present times. It is a paradox of our age that as we have become ever more individual, we also long to feel membered in community. The bindings that united people in the past, such as blood ties, nationality, societal roles, gender, religion, or race, have been loosening as individualism has grown. Can we still appreciate these aspects of difference without letting them block us from knowing and valuing our spiritual essence and our connections? While isolation and loneliness may come as shadows of our emerging individual selves, what also arises in ever more people is the will to find new ways of understanding and evolving our interconnectedness with all that is around us, with other human beings, with plants and animals, clouds, wind and sunshine, and the soil beneath our feet. Sophia holds this paradox of the individual and the community in her all-embracing wisdom, encouraging us in ways we may slowly comprehend, to lift her veil and make space in ourselves for otherness, for nature and spirit, and for love.

I don't expect agreement on my various musings, but I offer them with the wish that you will honor your own questions and ponderings. Questions of inner growth, of spiritual striving, of how to bear the suffering in the world without going under, and perhaps most of all, of how to love, often present themselves surrounded by veils. In acknowledging a question, the veil may begin to shift. Our questions matter; bringing them to consciousness, exploring them with others, waiting with an open heart for the spirit to speak—this is the ongoing work of unveiling.

> We learn to ask questions only when we are able to develop the inner balance that allows reverence and devotion to be retained when it comes to the sacred spheres of life, and when we are able to have an element in us that always seeks to remain independent of even our own judgement in relation to anything that comes to us from those spheres...not judging but asking questions, not only of people who may be able to tell us, but above all of the world of the spirit. We should face that world not with our opinions but with our questions, indeed in a questioning mood and attitude. (Rudolf Steiner)[39]

Appendix: The Foundation Stone Meditation

BY RUDOLF STEINER

Human soul!
You live within the limbs
Which bear you through the world of space
Into the spirit's ocean-being:
Practice spirit-recalling
In depths of soul,
Where in the wielding
World-Creator-Being
Your own I
Comes into being
In the I of God;
And you will truly live
In human world-all being.

For the Father-Spirit of the heights holds sway
In depths of worlds, begetting life.
Spirits of Strength:
Let ring forth from the heights
What in the depths is echoed,
Speaking:
Out of the Godhead we are born.
This is heard by the spirits of the elements
In east, west, north, south:
May human beings hear it!

Human soul!
You live within the beat of heart and lung
Which leads you through the rhythms
of time
Into the feeling of your own soul-being:
Practice spirit-sensing
In balance of the soul,
Where the surging deeds
Of world-evolving
Unite
Your own I
With the I of the world;
And you will truly feel
In human soul's creating.

For the Christ-will encircling us holds sway
In world rhythms, bestowing grace upon souls.
Spirits of Light:
Let from the east be enkindled
What through the west takes on form,
Speaking:
In Christ death becomes life.
This is heard by the spirits of the elements
In east, west, north, south:
May human beings hear it!

Human soul!
You live within the resting head
Which from the grounds of eternity
Unlocks for you world-thoughts:
Practice spirit-beholding
In stillness of thought,
Where the gods' eternal aims
Bestow
The light of cosmic being
On your own I
For free and active willing;
And you will truly think
In human spirit depths.

For the Spirit's world-thoughts hold sway
In cosmic being, imploring light.
Spirits of Soul:
Let from the depths be entreated
What in the heights will be heard,
Speaking:
In the spirit's world thoughts the soul awakens.
This is heard by the spirits of the elements
In east, west, north, south:
May human beings hear it!

At the turning point of time
The spirit-light of the world
Entered the earthly stream of being.
Darkness of night
Had ceased its reign;
Day-radiant light
Shone forth in human souls;
Light
That gives warmth
To simple shepherds' hearts;
Light
That enlightens
The wise heads of kings.

Light divine,
Christ-Sun,
Warm
Our hearts;
Enlighten
Our heads;
That good may become
What from our hearts
We are founding,
What from our heads
We direct
With focused will.

Bibliography

Bachofen, J. J. *Myth, Religion and Mother Right*. Princeton University, 1992.

Baring, Anne, and Jules Cashford. *The Myth of the Goddess: Evolution of an Image*. Arkana/Penguin, 1993.

Bock, Emil. *Threefold Mary*. SteinerBooks, 2003.

Debus, Michael. *Mary and Sophia*. Floris Books, 2013.

Eisenstein, Charles. *What is the Next Story?*, online essay, 01/09/2023.

Georgieff, Stephanie. *The Black Madonna*. Outskirts Press, 2016.

Harvey, Andrew, and Anne Baring. *The Divine Feminine*. Godsfield Press, 1996.

Matthews, Caitlin. *Sophia—Goddess of Wisdom*. Aquarian Press, 1992.

McDermott, Robert. "Rudolf Steiner on Sophia," in D. Banerji & R. McDermott. *Philo-Sophia: Wisdom Goddess Traditions*. Lotus Press, 2021

Neumann, Erich. *The Great Mother: An Analysis of the Archetype* (rev. ed.). Princeton University, 2015.

Pagels, Elaine. *The Gnostic Gospels*. Random House, 1979.

Paxino, Iris. *Bridges between Life and Death*. Floris Books, 2021

Powell, Robert. *The Sophia Teachings: The Emergence of the Divine Feminine in Our Time*. Lindisfarne Books, 2007.

Prokofieff, Sergei O. *The Heavenly Sophia and the Being Anthroposophia*. Temple Lodge, 1996.

Raff, Jeffrey. *The Wedding of Sophia*. Nicolas-Hays, Inc, 2003.

Robinson, James M. (ed). *The Nag Hammadi Library*. Brill, 1977.

Roy, Arundhati. *Azadi: Freedom. Fascism. Fiction*. Haymarket Books, 2020.

Schaefer, Signe Eklund. *Why on Earth? Biography and the Practice of Human Becoming*. SteinerBooks, 2013.

Schaefer, Signe Eklund, Margli Matthews, Betty Staley. *Ariadne's Awakening: Taking up the Threads of Consciousness*. Hawthorn Press, 1986.

Schipflinger, Thomas. *Sophia-Maria: A Holistic Vision of Creation.* Weiser, 1998.

Simard, Suzanne. *Finding the Mother Tree: Discovering the Wisdom of the Forest.* Knopf, 2021.

Steiner, Rudolf. *Ancient Myths and the New Isis Mystery.* SteinerBooks, 2018.

———. *Anthroposophical Leading Thoughts: Anthroposophy as a Path of Knowledge: The Michael Mystery.* Rudolf Steiner Press, 1973.

———. *The Archangel Michael: His Mission and Ours* (ed. Christopher Bamford). Anthroposophic Press, 1994.

———. *Awakening to Community.* Anthroposophic Press, 1974.

———. *The Fifth Gospel: From the Akashic Record.* Rudolf Steiner Press, 1978.

———. *The Goddess: From Natura to Divine Sophia.* Rudolf Steiner Press, 2002.

———. *The Gospel of John.* SteinerBooks, 2022.

———. *How to Know Higher Worlds: A Modern Path of Initiation.* Anthroposophic Press, 1994.

———. *Intuitive Thinking as a Spiritual Path: A Philosophy of Freedom.* Anthroposophic Press, 1995.

———. *Isis Mary Sophia: Her Mission and Ours* (ed. Christopher Bamford). SteinerBooks, 2003.

———. *The Michael Mystery* (trans. Marjorie Spock). SteinerBooks, 1984.

———. *The Mission of the Archangel Michael.* The Anthroposophic Press, 1961.

———. *An Outline of Esoteric Science.* Anthroposophic Press, 1997.

———. *Universal Spirituality and Human Physicality: Bridging the Divide: The Search for the New Isis and the Divine Sophia.* Rudolf Steiner Press, 2014.

Turkle, Sherry. *The Empathy Diaries.* Penguin, 2021.

Uhlein, Gabriele. *Meditations with Hildegard of Bingen.* Bear and Company, 1983.

Wall Kimmerer, Robin, *Braiding Sweetgrass: Indigenous Wisdom, Scientific Knowledge, and the Teachings of Plants.* Milkweed Editions, 2013.

Zeylmans Van Emmichoven, F. W. *The Foundation Stone.* Rudolf Steiner Press, London, 1963.

Acknowledgments

The ideas in this book have been growing in me for decades. Family members and friends now no longer living nurtured the beginnings of my questions, and I have gratefully felt their continuing support. Special thanks to Linda Norris and Patti Smith.

Several years ago, after a course I gave on feminine and masculine in the evolution of consciousness, Joseph Rubano asked me if I might write down what I had shared. This book is not really that, but thank you Joseph for planting the seed to tell Sophia's story. I am also grateful to my many students over the years for the ways we shared questions about Sophia, and to the Beholding Sophia Group of the Anthroposophical Society for our collective attention to Sophia's reality.

As I worked on this book, many friends, including several who do not share my long interest in Sophia, have encouraged me to wonder out loud, have generously engaged in rich conversations, and have asked me helpful, if sometimes difficult, questions. Thank you to Dede Bark, Stephanie Cooper, Maria de Zwaan, Yvonne Forman, Karen Gierlach, Roberta and Steven Haas. Jan Hutchinson, Noela Maletz, Carrie Schuchardt, Susan Shurtleff, Robin Zeamer, and many others. Some offered references, quotes, or poems; special thanks to Gloria Kemp for alerting me to Thomas Merton. Deep gratitude to those who also read part or all of the manuscript, offering helpful, challenging, and supportive comments: Kathleen Bowen, Jennifer Brooks Quinn, Margli Matthews, Davina Muse, Robert McDermott, and Patricia Rubano.

John Scott Legg expressed interest after hearing the barest of an idea and was encouraging all along the way. I am very grateful to be publishing with SteinerBooks. Of course, I am deeply grateful to Rudolf Steiner for a lifetime of inspiration.

My daughter Karin Schaefer offered one of her paintings for the cover, which makes me very happy. I thank her and my son Stefan Schaefer, as well as their partners Diane Crespo and Chenta Laury for their generous hearts and the ongoing interweaving of our lives.

And Chris, I have such gratitude for all our years together and, lately, for all the ways you have supported this book—letting me sound out ideas, reading drafts, asking important questions, and continuing to assure me that I should go on. Thank you for all that and so much more!

Endnotes

1 Rudolf Steiner, *The Gospel of John,* ch. 12.

2 *Ariadne's Awakening: Taking Up the Threads of Consciousness,* with chapters by Margli Matthews, Betty Staley, and me. We explored the need for balance between feminine and masculine forces within the individual, in society, and also within the evolution of human consciousness. A further look at this challenge is elaborated in chapters 2 and 10 of my book *Why on Earth? Biography and the Practice of Human Becoming.*

3 F. W. Zeylmans van Emmichoven, *The Foundation Stone.*

4 Current, complete edition: *Universal Spirituality and Human Physicality: Bridging the Divide: The Search for the New Isis and the Divine Sophia,* lect. 15, vol. 202 in the Collected Works (CW). See also Rudolf Steiner, *Isis Mary Sophia: Her Mission and Ours,* a collection edited by Christopher Bamford. I also recount and reflect on the myth in chapter 10 of my book *Why on Earth?*

5 Rudolf Steiner, "Ancient Myths" in *Isis Mary Sophia.*

6 "Ancient Myths," op cit, p 66.

7 Anne Baring and Jules Cashford, *The Myth of the Goddess: Evolution of an Image,* p. 176.

8 Apuleius, *The Golden Ass,* quoted in op. cit., p. 278.

9 The Myth of the Goddess, op. cit., p. 264.

10 Op. cit., p. 28.

11 Op. cit., p. 303.

12 Aeschylus, *The Eumenides,* quoted in op. cit., p. 337.

13 *The Myth of the Goddess,* op. cit., p. 506.

14 Rudolf Steiner, *The Fifth Gospel,* especially ch. 7, 8, 9.

15 *The Myth of the Goddess,* op. cit., pp. 630–631.

16 Op. cit., p. 620.

17 Rudolf Steiner, "Search for the New Isis, Divine Sophia," in *Isis Mary Sophia,* p. 211.

18 *Isis Mary Sophia,* op. cit., p. 35.

19 *The Myth of the Goddess,* op. cit., pp. 640–641.

20 Op. cit., p 649.

21 Sherry Turkle, *The Empathy Diaries,* p. 335–337.

22 Many spiritual teachers speak of this, including Rudolf Steiner, *How to Know Higher Worlds.*

23 Center for Biography and Social Art (biographysocialart.org).

24 Iris Paxino, *Bridges between Life and Death,* p. 7.

25 Steiner speaks in many places of what he calls Luciferic and Ahrimanic beings who would pull us off center, pull us away from the true light of the Christ Being. The struggle goes on in each of us, and in our social order. See for example, *The Mission of the Archangel Michael,* pp. 7–9.

26 "Pandemic Is a Portal," Yes!, April 17, 2020, from Arundhati Roy, Azadi: *Freedom. Fascism. Fiction.*

27 Charles Eisenstein, "What Is the Next Story?" (online essay, 01/09/2023).

28 Rudolf Steiner, *The Fifth Gospel: From the Akashic Record.*

29 Rudolf Steiner, "The Search for the New Isis, Divine Sophia," in *Isis Mary Sophia.*

30 Robert McDermott, "Rudolf Steiner on Sophia," in Banerji and McDermott, *Philo-Sophia: Wisdom Goddess Traditions,* p 262.

31 Rudolf Steiner, *Awakening to Community,* p. 61.

32 Signe Eklund Schaefer, "A Sophia Mosaic," *Being Human,* winter/spring 2021.

33 Rudolf Steiner, "The Being Anthroposophia," Berlin, 2/3/1913; in *Isis, Mary, Sophia,* op. cit.; pp. 125–126.

34 F. W. Zeylmans van Emmichoven, *The Foundation Stone.*

35 Translation of the Foundation Stone Meditation used here is by members of the Speech Association of North America

36 Rudolf Steiner spoke and wrote extensively on questions of spiritual practice; see, for example, *How to Know Higher Worlds* or *An Outline of Esoteric Science,* ch. 4. For a practical look at the three practices of the Foundation Stone verse, see my book *Why on Earth?* chap. 9.

37 Rudolf Steiner, "The Nature of the Virgin Sophia and of the Holy Spirit," in *Isis Mary Sophia,* op. cit.; p. 73.

38 Sergei O. Prokofieff, *The Heavenly Sophia and the Being Anthroposophia,* pp. 103–104.

39 Rudolf Steiner, *The Fifth Gospel,* op. cit., pp. 150–151.